W9-BJH-118

365 PRAYERS
FOR A
Woman of
GOD

365 PRAYERS FOR A Woman of GOD

BARBOUR BOOKS
An Imprint of Barbour Publishing, Inc.

ISBN 978-1-64352-406-1

Prayers originally published in *180 Prayers for a Hopeful Heart, 3-Minute Prayers for Women* and *180 Prayers for a Woman of God*, all published by Barbour Publishing.

Published by Barbour Books, an imprint of Barbour Publishing, Inc., 1810 Barbour Drive, Uhrichsville, Ohio 44683, www.barbourbooks.com

Our mission is to inspire the world with the life-changing message of the Bible.

Member of the
Evangelical Christian
Publishers Association

Printed in China.

Be still before the LORD.

PSALM 37:7 NIV

The all-powerful God we serve is interested in you. In fact, He longs to hear your prayers. You are welcome—any time—to bring any petition before the King of the universe. Now that's genuine love!

These encouraging daily prayers are especially for those times when you are weary from the busyness of everyday life and your soul is longing for a quiet time of refreshment in the heavenly Creator's calming presence. Although this book isn't meant as a tool for deep Bible study, each soul-stirring prayer can be a touchstone to keep you grounded and focused on the One who hears all your prayers. May this book remind you that the heavenly Father cares about everything you have to say. Go on...talk to Him today. He's ready and waiting to hear from you!

DAY 1
Through the Waters

Lord, there have been so many "deep water" situations in my life. Many times, I felt as if I would drown. I nearly lost sight of Your plans for my life. "Tomorrow" felt like an elusive dream. Thank You for the reminder that the things I'm walking through will not consume me. I won't drown, even with the swirling floodwaters threatening to take me down. You have declared this over my life, Father, and I am grateful for Your assurance that I can make it through any situation, good or bad. Amen.

"When you pass through the waters, I will be with you; and when you pass through the rivers, they will not sweep over you. When you walk through the fire, you will not be burned; the flames will not set you ablaze."

ISAIAH 43:2 NIV

DAY 2
Prospering in the Valley

I've walked through some dark valleys, Father. I know You were there, because I sensed the times You carried me. I don't claim to understand the difficult seasons, Lord. I wish they were fewer and farther between. But there is comfort in knowing that the valleys are easier to navigate now that I understand I'm not alone. You can even show me how to prosper (i.e., do well) during hard seasons. Thank You for never leaving me, and please show me how to be a better friend to those who are walking through valleys today. Amen.

Even when I walk through the darkest valley,
I will not be afraid, for you are close beside me.
Your rod and your staff protect and comfort me.

PSALM 23:4 NLT

DAY 3
Grace for Everything

Father, I'm thankful for Your grace—Your unmerited favor to me through Jesus Christ, and that special strength You give Your child in times of need, trial, and temptation. If not for Your grace, I wouldn't even be able to approach You. Thank You for extending favor to me: forgiving my sins and adopting me into Your family. And thank You so much for that extra dose of perseverance that You keep giving to me in tough situations. I'm so thankful Your resource center will never experience a shortage. I praise You today for grace. Amen.

He gives us more grace.

JAMES 4:6 NIV

DAY 4
Glorifying God in My Work

God, today as I work both in my home and outside of it, may my attitude glorify You. I am not of this world, but I am in it, and often it has too much influence on me. May I think twice before I grumble, Father, about the tasks set before me this day. I will choose to work as unto my Father, and may my countenance reflect Your love to those around me. Amen.

And whatsoever ye do, do it heartily, as to the Lord, and not unto men; knowing that of the Lord ye shall receive the reward of the inheritance; for ye serve the Lord Christ.
Colossians 3:23–24 kjv

DAY 5
He Will Fulfill

So many projects around my house are unfinished, Lord. My intentions are good, but my desire to carry through often wanes. Not so with You. You always fulfill Your purposes. If You start something in my life, I can trust You to complete it. May I learn from Your example, Father. I don't just want to be someone who "gets off to a great start." Lord, I long to be a person who finishes well. Help me as I strive to become more like You, Father. Amen.

The LORD will fulfill his purpose for me;
your steadfast love, O LORD, endures forever.
Do not forsake the work of your hands.

PSALM 138:8 ESV

DAY 6
Abounding in Love

If anyone had told me I'd be this loved, Father, I'm not sure I would have believed them. From the time I was a little girl, I yearned for love. So many times, I was disappointed. People act loving but turn on a dime, their affections waning. You, Lord? You've never changed. You were abounding in love the day I met You and continue to pour out affections. Even when I wander down the wrong road or make mistakes, there You are, loving me still. Praise You for Your goodness to me, Father. My soul prospers because of Your great love. Amen.

Lord, You are kind and forgiving and have
great love for those who call to you.
PSALM 86:5 NCV

DAY 7
Joyful in Hope

God, the longer I live, the more I realize that joy and hope go hand in hand. I have joy because my hope is in You. Thank You, Lord, that as Your daughter, I do not go out to face the day in hopelessness. No matter what happens, I can find joy because my hope is not in this world or in my circumstances. My hope is in the Lord. Amen.

Happy is he that hath the God of Jacob for his help,
whose hope is in the LORD his God.

PSALM 146:5 KJV

DAY 8
Life's Security System

Father, I deal with a phobia. It isn't anything life-threatening, but it's embarrassing. I haven't told anyone, and I'm hoping I never have to. But I ask You now to help me; I don't want my phobia to keep me from living the life You've planned for me. Help me to bring this fear to You; show me that You are in control, that You are the security system in my life. I ask this in Jesus' name, amen.

For the Spirit God gave us does not make us timid, but gives us power, love and self-discipline.
2 Timothy 1:7 niv

DAY 9
Your Will Is Perfect

Your Word tells me that I need to pray for Your will to be done, Father. It's not always easy, I'll admit. When I ponder the notion that I need to bend my will to Yours, I realize it all comes down to one word: *trust*. If I can really grab hold of the truth that You will never harm me, that You are only looking out for my good, then I can trust that Your will is perfect. Thinking like this is a new thing for me, I must admit. But I'm learning that Your will (even when it does not match my own) is good and pleasing and perfect! How could I say no to that? I trust You, Lord. Amen.

Do not be shaped by this world; instead be changed within by a new way of thinking. Then you will be able to decide what God wants for you; you will know what is good and pleasing to him and what is perfect.

ROMANS 12:2 NCV

DAY 10
What We Hope For

A good father knows his children. He knows not just their outward appearance but their longings and desires. He knows what little Johnny is hoping to unwrap under the Christmas tree and that little Susie is looking forward to a Tinkerbell party. In short, he knows their hopes. The same is true with You, Father. You know the things I'm wishing and hoping for. You know when I'm hoping to get that next pay raise or new job. You can see into my heart when I'm longing to be a better parent or wife. You know what I'm hoping for. And I'm so grateful, Father! Amen.

Faith means being sure of the things we hope for and knowing that something is real even if we do not see it.
HEBREWS 11:1 NCV

DAY 11
Instant Gratification

Dear Lord, so many things are instantaneous in my world. From fast food to instant credit, we can satisfy our penchant for immediate gratification at every juncture. But I have to keep reminding myself that You often work by process. When it comes to the work You're doing in me, You use the steady maturing of Your Word within me to make me more like Jesus. You, the master Gardener, water the seeds, prune the unnecessary limbs, and watch over me carefully as the fruit of my life continues to ripen. Instead of being impatient, I aim to revel in Your timely and tender loving care. Amen.

But grow in grace, and in the knowledge of our Lord and Saviour Jesus Christ.

2 Peter 3:18 kjv

DAY 12
You Know the Heart

Only You know the motivations of others, Lord. I question people all the time—wondering where their hearts are, wondering why they do the things they do. Why they choose to hurt others. Why they fall down on the job. Why they don't follow through. Why they break promises. It's not mine to question, Father, but to trust that You will speak to the deepest places in their hearts. I can trust You to know what's going on, deep inside each of us. I praise You for that! Amen.

"Forgive and act; deal with everyone according to all they do, since you know their hearts (for you alone know every human heart), so that they will fear you all the time they live in the land you gave our ancestors."
1 Kings 8:39–40 niv

DAY 13
Made from the Invisible

Life is like a giant puzzle to me at times, Lord, only the puzzle pieces aren't always clear. Sometimes I feel like I'm groping around in the dark, trying to force things together. I can't always get the pieces to fit. Oh, but You have the perfect plan all prepared in advance. There's no need to force anything, is there? What I can't see, You can. When I can't fit the invisible pieces together, You shuffle the board in Your own creative way and make things crystal clear so that I only move when I feel led by Your Spirit. Trusting when my vision isn't clear isn't always easy, but You make it worth it, Father. Thank You! Amen.

By faith we understand that the universe was formed at God's command, so that what is seen was not made out of what was visible.

HEBREWS 11:3 NIV

DAY 14
Claim Peace

Father, peace is an elusive emotion. So many people talk about peace, but few can claim it. You promised to give us Your peace, a calm assurance that You are present and sovereign in all our ways. I want more of this peace every day. Although there are many upsetting things in my world, Your peace will help me cope with them all. Amid Your peace, I am neither troubled nor afraid, merely allowing myself to bask in Your presence. Amen.

"Peace I leave with you, My peace I give to you."
JOHN 14:27 NKJV

DAY 15
He's in Control

Thank You, Lord, that You have a perfect plan for my life. I know I don't always understand it, but You know what's best, and everything that happens is for a reason—that You might be glorified. I'm so glad that You are in control and that I need not worry. Amen.

There are many devices in a man's heart;
nevertheless the counsel of the LORD, that shall stand.
PROVERBS 19:21 KJV

DAY 16
Sensory Joys

Dear God, thank You for the five senses—sight, sound, touch, smell, and taste. You could have designed a virtual world, but instead You created one that can be experienced. Today I want to revel in the fact that I'm alive. I want to delight in the tactile joys I often take for granted. I'm grateful for each one. Amen.

For in him we live, and move, and have our being.
ACTS 17:28 KJV

DAY 17
The Light Shines

I've been in situations that felt hopeless, Lord. It was almost as if the light had gone out and I was surrounded by utter darkness. Whenever I've been that low, any glimmer of daylight served to bring hope. Now I see that You're the one who opens the eyes of my heart. You bring light to dark situations. You're the one who reminds me of the calling on my life, even when I'm in a low spot, because You know that a ripple of hope will wash over me at the reminder. I'm so glad these low places don't last long, Father. Thank You for bringing hope in my darkest hour. Amen.

The light shines in the darkness,
and the darkness has not overcome it.
JOHN 1:5 ESV

DAY 18
His Workmanship

Oh, how I love this verse, Father! I picture You as a wood-carver, Lord, shaping me into a thing of beauty. Your Son, Jesus, is the model, and You are carving His image as my life moves along. I would imagine there are some seasons where I stubbornly refuse to be molded. Forgive me for those times, Lord. I want to be pliable in Your hands, someone You can be proud of. What an honor to be Your workmanship, Lord. You are the Master Artist, after all, and I submit myself to the process, Your willing child. Amen.

For we are his workmanship, created in Christ Jesus for good works, which God prepared beforehand, that we should walk in them.

EPHESIANS 2:10 ESV

DAY 19
A Glimpse Inside

I'm so grateful for the times when You pull back the curtain, Lord, and give me tiny glimpses into Your plans for my life. I can hardly comprehend the magnificence of Your thought process, but Your love is overwhelming during these "glimpsing" seasons. What a privilege to walk through life with Your hand so tightly clasped in my own. What a joy to know that I can trust You implicitly. And how generous and kind You are, Lord. All You ask is that I call on You, so today I choose to do that with my whole heart. Amen.

"Call to me and I will answer you and tell you great and unsearchable things you do not know."

JEREMIAH 33:3 NIV

DAY 20
Time Management

Dear God, sometimes I think I need more than twenty-four hours in my day! It seems I never have enough time. I think with longing about simpler seasons in my life when I could actually complete my to-do lists. There was such satisfaction in having a few stress-free moments. Now, my schedule is filled, and I'm so harried. Holy Spirit, please guide me in this area of my life. How I use my time is part of stewardship, so I'm asking for Your wisdom. Show me how to manage the hours I have so I can honor You in everything I do. In Christ's name, amen.

Teach us to number our days,
that we may gain a heart of wisdom.
PSALM 90:12 NIV

DAY 21
With All My Heart

Here's a little confession, Lord: I often do things half-heartedly. Housework. Laundry. Tasks at my job. This is difficult to admit, but I don't always give my relationship with You 100 percent either. Of course, You already know that. You see my motivation (or lack thereof). I'm so sorry, Father. It feels good to make that confession because I want to be an "all-in" sort of girl, one who seeks You with my whole heart. Give me the push I need, even when I don't feel like it, Lord. Amen.

"Then you will call on me and come and pray to me,
and I will listen to you. You will seek me and find
me when you seek me with all your heart."
JEREMIAH 29:12–13 NIV

DAY 22
That Your Joy May Be Full

It gives me great joy to plan things, Lord. Christmas dinner, parties, family gatherings—I love putting those plans together. And I do it all with others in mind. I can envision the looks on their faces as they partake of the foods I've made, the packages I've wrapped. What joy it must bring You to create plans for my life. Thank You for allowing that joy to spill over as I walk out the path You have laid for me. You've done it all with me in mind, and I'm forever grateful. Praise You, Father! Amen.

"I have told you this so that my joy may be in you and that your joy may be complete."

JOHN 15:11 NIV

DAY 23
Fixing My Thoughts

God, today I'm having a pity party. My thoughts are so focused on earthly things that I am having trouble looking up. I could mope around here all day, but I guess it's time for the music to stop and the party to end. Lord, You can't work through me when I'm feeling sorry for myself. Forgive me for my pettiness, and let me respond to life with maturity. Help me to focus on good, praiseworthy things. In Christ's name, amen.

Fix your thoughts on what is true, and honorable, and right, and pure, and lovely, and admirable.

PHILIPPIANS 4:8 NLT

DAY 24
A Godly Example

God, help me to be an example of a faithful disciple of Christ to my family and friends. Those who are close in our lives have the ability to lead us toward or away from righteousness and godliness. I pray that all I do and say will honor You and that I will never be a stumbling block to others. May all within my sphere of influence find me faithful to You. Amen.

The righteous is more excellent than his neighbour:
but the way of the wicked seduceth them.

PROVERBS 12:26 KJV

DAY 25
Gossip

Lord, I got caught in gossip today. I didn't mean to though. A group of us were just talking about this and that, and You know how women are. We're so into relationships and what others are doing. Before long, the conversation had dug itself a little too deep into someone else's life. I tried to stop listening but didn't try hard enough. By the time we broke up our little gabfest, I felt terribly guilty. Please forgive me, Father. Give me the courage to make the right decision next time; help me refuse to listen to negative stories about someone who is not there to defend him- or herself. In Jesus' name, amen.

Let all. . .evil speaking be put away
from you, with all malice.
EPHESIANS 4:31 NKJV

DAY 26
Good Not Evil

I wish the word *enemies* had never been invented, Father. I know, I know—You didn't come up with such a divisive notion. Your enemy, Satan, did. I've experienced division in my life, Lord, and it doesn't feel good. Not one little bit. But it brings me great comfort to know that You are preparing a table before me in the presence of the very people who rise up against me. This is part of Your great plan for my life, to guard me from those who would seek to do me harm. I'm so grateful for Your protection, Father! Amen.

You prepare a meal for me in front of my enemies.
PSALM 23:5 NCV

DAY 27
An Earnest Reward

I've never been much for dieting, Lord. It's never fun to sacrifice things I love. Oh, but the rewards can be amazing. It's so much fun to look at before-and-after photos when I've dropped a few pounds. Is that how You feel sometimes, Lord? Do You look at my spiritual before-and-after photos and smile? (I hope I'm progressing in the right direction!) The rewards of seeking You are mine for the taking, but I don't serve You for what I can get out of it. I continue to grow in my relationship with You, Father, because I adore You. I want to please You in all that I do. Amen.

It is impossible to please God without faith. Anyone who wants to come to him must believe that God exists and that he rewards those who sincerely seek him.

HEBREWS 11:6 NLT

My Portion, My Hope

I know what it's like to be full after a tasty meal, Lord. I've been there plenty of times, especially during the holidays. There's a level of satisfaction when the portion is just right. I've found the same to be true in my relationship with You. You are all I'll ever need. You fill me up on days when I'm feeling empty. You bring hope on days when I'm in crisis. You are truly my all in all, Father. Praise You for that. Amen.

"The LORD is my portion," says my soul,
"therefore I will hope in him."
LAMENTATIONS 3:24 ESV

DAY 29
We Know in Part

I'll admit it, Lord—there have been times in my life when I've acted like a know-it-all. I've tried to show up others or prove they were wrong and I was right. I must confess that I don't know it all, Father. Only You can claim that. I know in part. You know in full. It boggles my mind to think about the scope of Your knowledge, especially when it comes to the plans You've made for my life. I trust not in what I do or don't know, but in You, the All-Knowing. You've got me covered, Father. Bless You for that! Amen.

For now we see only a reflection as in a mirror;
then we shall see face to face. Now I know in part;
then I shall know fully, even as I am fully known.

1 CORINTHIANS 13:12 NIV

DAY 30
Your Counsel Stands

Because You see all and know all, You can be trusted with not just my life but my family, my community, my state, my country—the whole of humankind, in fact. When the news on TV is bad, I can trust You, Father. When things are falling apart politically, You're still on the throne. You know best how to reach the hearts of those who need change, Father. Help me release any anxieties and rest in the knowledge that You know and You care. Your counsel stands, Lord. How mighty You are! Amen.

Declaring the end from the beginning, and from ancient times the things that are not yet done, saying, My counsel shall stand, and I will do all my pleasure.

Isaiah 46:10 KJV

DAY 31
Fear No Evil

How wonderful, God, that death has no power over the Christian! You are a strong and mighty God, the one true God. You are with me, protecting me all the way. And when the end of this life comes, whenever that may be, You will walk with me through the valley of the shadow of death. Death has lost its sting because Christ has conquered it! In Your name I pray, amen.

Yea, though I walk through the valley of the shadow of death, I will fear no evil: for thou art with me; thy rod and thy staff they comfort me.

PSALM 23:4 KJV

DAY 32
Music

Dear Lord, music is the universal language of the human family. Today, music is available on a multitude of electronic devices. And there are so many genres—an array of listening options. Some appeal to me; others don't. But I want to base my choices on Your principles. What I listen to will affect my mood, my attitude, and my spiritual state of being. Holy Spirit, give me discernment. Let the music to which I listen not go counter to what You're trying to do in me. Amen.

Whatsoever ye do, do all to the glory of God.
1 Corinthians 10:31 KJV

DAY 33
Lessons in Trust

Heavenly Father, teach me to trust. I know it's an area of weakness for me. In spite of the fact that I know Your character and Your track record, I find it so difficult to relinquish to You the important areas of life. Oh, I say that I will, and I do put forth effort to rely on You, but we both know that, in my heart, I find it hard to let You handle everything. So take my hand, Lord, and teach me to trust. You're the Master; I am forever Your student. In Christ's name, amen.

I have put my trust in the Lord GOD,
that I may declare all Your works.
PSALM 73:28 NKJV

DAY 34
Too Wonderful

So many things seem over my head, Lord. They are above me. When it comes to Your ways, Your Word, Your plans, I guess that's a good thing. If I understood Your ways, if I could comprehend the things You comprehend, then my need for You would be very small, wouldn't it? Oh, but I do need You, Father, and not just because of my lack of understanding. I stand in awe of who You are, Lord, and gaze on Your greatness with awe and wonder. You are too wonderful, Father! Amen.

Such knowledge is too wonderful for me,
too lofty for me to attain.
PSALM 139:6 NIV

DAY 35
You Make Precious Promises

I love listening when You speak, Lord, especially when You reiterate the promises found in Your Word. Oh, how I love them! You've promised never to leave me or forsake me. You've promised to send the Holy Spirit to comfort me in times of need. You've promised that You will meet all my needs according to Your riches in glory. Through these and hundreds of other promises, I see glimpses of Your divine nature. Thank You that Your promises are true. Amen.

And because of his glory and excellence, he has given us great and precious promises. These are the promises that enable you to share his divine nature and escape the world's corruption caused by human desires.

2 PETER 1:4 NLT

DAY 36
That All Might Be Saved

Of all the plans You've set in motion, Lord, this one's my favorite. It is Your good and perfect will that all will be saved. All—everyone! People across this beautiful planet are all loved by You (even people who are radically different from me). Thank You for including me in the plan to reach people with the Gospel, Father. May I be an example to all of Your love, Your grace, Your peace. And while I'm waiting for those around me to come to a knowledge of the truth, may I exemplify Your gracious heart toward them. Amen.

This is good, and pleases God our Savior,
who wants all people to be saved and to
come to a knowledge of the truth.
1 TIMOTHY 2:3–4 NIV

Praying for Bold Faith

I desire a bold faith, Jesus. Like the woman who followed You, crying out, asking that You cast a demon from her daughter. She was a Gentile, not a Jew; yet she called You the "Son of David." She acknowledged You as the Messiah. And You stopped. Her faith impressed You. You healed the child. May I be so bold. May I recognize that You are the only solution to every problem. Amen.

Then Jesus answered and said unto her, O woman,
great is thy faith: be it unto thee even as thou wilt.
And her daughter was made whole from that very hour.
MATTHEW 15:28 KJV

DAY 38
The Same Old Me

Lord, today I come to You a bit discouraged. The traits I see in myself are ones I don't like. It seems I could do much more for You without some of the inherent flaws of my personality. So help me overcome my defects or use me in spite of them. Help me to love myself, as imperfect as I am, and to strive to be the best me I can be. I know You can find a way around my impediments and use me for Your glory, just like You used Moses in spite of his speech problem. Amen.

You have searched me, LORD, and you know me.
PSALM 139:1 NIV

DAY 39
A Perfect Place

Creator God, I wish there weren't diseases in our world. Those tiny microbes that infiltrate the immune system are responsible for so much pain and grief. Although sickness was not present in the Garden of Eden—that perfect place You intended for us—it is a part of this life now, a consequence of the curse under which our world suffers. But someday You'll create a new earth, and I know bacteria won't stand a chance there. I look forward to that, Father God, for then the world will once again be "very good." Amen.

Now I saw a new heaven and a new earth, for the first heaven and the first earth had passed away.

REVELATION 21:1 NKJV

DAY 40
Invitation to Rest

Jesus, You told Your disciples to rest. You directed them to leave the crowd and to relax and eat. You saw that they had been busy with ministry and they needed to recuperate. If You directed them to rest, even these twelve who worked at Your side daily, You must want me to rest as well. Remind me to take breaks from ministry. I needed to hear that You give me permission to rest! Amen.

He said unto them, Come ye yourselves apart into a desert place, and rest a while: for there were many coming and going, and they had no leisure so much as to eat.

MARK 6:31 KJV

DAY 41
Full to the Brim

Father, what an amazing picture You have painted with this verse. Your knowledge is too lofty for me. I cannot attain it. But I can picture it spread out like mighty rushing waters across this planet, covering vast areas. My thoughts hardly compare to Yours. They are minute in comparison. But You invite me to share glimpses, to see that Your ways—though higher—are better for me than my own. How could I not trust a God who sees all, knows all, and guides all? I trust You, Lord. Amen.

For the earth shall be full of the knowledge of the LORD, as the waters cover the sea.
ISAIAH 11:9 KJV

DAY 42
In Christ's Strength

Father, I am so thankful for the strength that is mine as a Christian. I cannot do anything on my own, but through Christ, I can do all things. It is comforting to know that the word *all* includes the trials and concerns that I bring to You this morning. I lay them at Your feet, Lord. I take You at Your Word. I can do all things through Jesus who lives in me. Amen.

I can do all things through Christ which strengtheneth me.
PHILIPPIANS 4:13 KJV

DAY 43
Protection from Temptation

There is temptation all around me, Father. It is easy for me to say no to some of them. But there are subtle ways that Satan tempts me also. The movie that isn't appropriate. . . but all my friends are going to see. The newest style that is cute and fun. . .but a bit provocative for a Christian woman. Lord, keep my heart focused on You. Protect my heart from the influences of this world. Amen.

Can a man take fire in his bosom,
and his clothes not be burned?

PROVERBS 6:27 KJV

DAY 44
God Hears My Prayers

Lord, the gods of other religions are not approachable. Their subjects bow before them in anguish, hoping to find favor in their sight. These gods are not real. You are the one true and living God, a loving heavenly Father. I love that Your Word says I can come before You with confidence. You hear my prayers. You know my heart. Thank You, Father. Speak to my heart as I meditate upon Your Word now. Amen.

This is the confidence that we have in him, that,
if we ask any thing according to his will, he heareth us.
1 John 5:14 KJV

DAY 45
Measuring Stick

It's remarkable to think about Your level of understanding, Father. It's beyond measure. You "get" it—all the time. There's never a situation You don't understand. There's never a problem You can't solve. There's never a relationship issue You can't navigate. There's never a question You can't answer. Oh, how I wish I had Your measuring stick, Lord. For now though, I'll lean on the fact that Your ability to move on my behalf is all I need. I'm so grateful for that, Lord! Amen.

Great is our Lord, and abundant in power;
his understanding is beyond measure.

PSALM 147:5 ESV

DAY 46
His Ways Are Higher

Your ways are higher, Lord. It's not always clear in the moment, but my plans—great as they might seem—don't even come close to Yours, simply because You see what I can't see. You know what I don't know. You care in ways I simply cannot comprehend. When the road You're leading me down makes no sense to my finite mind, Father, sweep in and remind me that Your thoughts, Your ways, are always higher. Amen.

"For my thoughts are not your thoughts,
neither are your ways my ways," declares the LORD.
ISAIAH 55:8 NIV

DAY 47
A Joyous Celebration

Father, every day can be a celebration when I walk in relationship with You! With my eyes tipped upward toward You, how can my heart help but sing? My focus on You brings joy. It brings peace, even when things around me are swirling. And if I need any reminders of what it's like to live in holy celebration, all I need to do is look around at nature. The very mountains are singing, even now. Trees are clapping their hands in praise. I join them in bringing honor to Your name, Father. Amen.

"You will live in joy and peace. The mountains and hills will burst into song, and the trees of the field will clap their hands! Where once there were thorns, cypress trees will grow. Where nettles grew, myrtles will sprout up. These events will bring great honor to the LORD's name; they will be an everlasting sign of his power and love."

Isaiah 55:12–13 NLT

DAY 48
Still Working on Me

Dear God, I'm a far cry from perfect, but I'm confident in the knowledge that You love me just as I am. You are the One who has begun a work in me, and You will be faithful to complete what has been started. What a thrill to know that You'll make me what You want me to be. Amen.

Let not mercy and truth forsake thee: bind them about thy neck; write them upon the table of thine heart.
PROVERBS 3:3 KJV

DAY 49
Balancing Work and Rest

I had to chuckle as I read the verse that says, "Give not sleep to thine eyes" (Proverbs 6:4 KJV). I guess I don't have much trouble obeying that! I have more difficulty with "Come. . .apart. . .and rest a while" (Mark 6:31 KJV). I think I'm getting the picture though. Please help me learn to balance work and rest. Amen.

My presence shall go with thee,
and I will give thee rest.
EXODUS 33:14 KJV

DAY 50
The Simple Life

Dear God, simplicity is a buzzword today. It seems everyone wants "simple" in some fashion. Perhaps it's because life has become too complicated for many of us; we yearn for a more laid-back lifestyle. Lord, I need to simplify my goals in my relationships and my work. Doing so will help me to have a more laser-like focus. And in my spiritual life, a little simplifying might be good too. Instead of trying to conquer large portions of scripture daily, help me to focus on a few verses, thus letting me steadily grow in understanding. Lord, help me keep simple goals and a simple faith as I simply live for You. Amen.

Aspire to lead a quiet life, to mind your own business, and to work with your own hands.
1 Thessalonians 4:11 nkjv

DAY 51

Prospering above the Circumstances

So many times, Lord, I live *under* my circumstances. I let them weigh me down. They dictate whether I move forward. Many times, I remain frozen in place, convinced there's no point in trying. You've asked me to live *above* my circumstances, not below them. With Your help, I can actually soar as free as an eagle. What a hopeful image that paints in my mind! Instead of allowing my challenges to cause weariness, I'll mount up with wings energized by Your Spirit—and off I'll go, stronger than ever. Thank You for lifting me, Lord. Amen.

Those who hope in the LORD will renew their strength.
They will soar on wings like eagles; they will run and
not grow weary, they will walk and not be faint.

ISAIAH 40:31 NIV

DAY 52
For My Sake

If I needed any additional proof that You want only good things for me, Father, I need look no further than Your Son. How sobering, to realize that He took the punishment for my sins. I deserved to be punished but received only good instead. It's remarkable to think that You would do anything for my sake. When I put this in perspective, Father, I realize that I should be doing everything for Your sake. What an amazing revelation. Today I commit myself to trying harder. May I focus more on Your will than my own, Lord. Help me? Amen.

He was wounded for the wrong we did; he was crushed for the evil we did. The punishment, which made us well, was given to him, and we are healed because of his wounds.
ISAIAH 53:5 NCV

DAY 53
Called to Shine

You've called me to shine Your light, Lord. That's an important part of Your plan for my life. Sometimes I feel the pressure of this too keenly. I want to be the best witness for You that I can be. I don't want my light to be a distraction to others; I want it to guide them to You. But I'm so flawed, Father. I make mistakes. Some days I'm like a flickering candle, about to burn out. Thank You for giving me multiple chances to shine, Lord. Light the flame once again, I pray. Amen.

"You are the light of the world. A town built on a hill cannot be hidden. Neither do people light a lamp and put it under a bowl. Instead they put it on its stand, and it gives light to everyone in the house. In the same way, let your light shine before others, that they may see your good deeds and glorify your Father in heaven."

MATTHEW 5:14–16 NIV

DAY 54
Fruit of the Spirit

I see how it is, Father—You want to prosper me from the inside out. What good would it do to lavish gifts on me if my heart wasn't in the right place? I would be like a spoiled child, demanding favors but never checking my attitude. Instead, You prosper my soul. You teach me how to live in peace. In joy. Exhibiting kindness, even to those who've hurt me. You prosper me by showing me how to remain faithful, even when I don't feel like it. And You're teaching me self-control, every step of the way. I love prospering from the inside out, Lord. Thank You! Amen.

But the fruit of the Spirit is love, joy, peace, forbearance, kindness, goodness, faithfulness, gentleness and self-control. Against such things there is no law.
GALATIANS 5:22–23 NIV

DAY 55
Starting Where I Am

Jesus, You give tall orders! How can I teach all nations and baptize people? Oh. . .you mean I might not even have to leave my community? There are people all around me who don't know You, Lord. Help me to start with those in my sphere of influence. The grocery store clerk who seems tired and distraught. . . The teacher at my child's school who is so lost. . . Give me the courage to reach out. Amen.

Go ye therefore, and teach all nations,
baptizing them in the name of the Father,
and of the Son, and of the Holy Ghost.
MATTHEW 28:19 KJV

DAY 56
Legacy

Dear God, what kind of legacy am I leaving? I want to be remembered as more than a woman who dressed nicely, had a great family, and went to church. I want to be remembered for the way I invested myself in the lives of others. After all, love is the only lasting thing on this earth, something that will remain when I am physically gone but living with You in eternity. Lord, let my legacy be wrapped up in serving others in love. In Jesus' name, amen.

Prophecy and speaking in unknown languages and special knowledge will become useless. But love will last forever!

1 Corinthians 13:8 nlt

DAY 57
The Real Me

Heavenly Father, so many people in my world wear masks. We earth dwellers are afraid to be real with others; we fear losing the respect and esteem of our peers. And, oddly enough, we're often afraid to be real with even You—and You know everything about us anyway. I want to be genuine in my approach and interaction with others, including You. Give me the courage to reject the lure of artificial "perfectness" and instead live out my life and relationships in a real way. Amen.

I have chosen the way of truth.

PSALM 119:30 NKJV

DAY 58
Provisions from God

God, there is no creature on earth You do not see or provide for. I'm bringing praise to You right now for the daily things You supply for me. It is through Your goodness that I have food to eat, clothes to wear, and water to drink. Help me always be thankful for what I have and not emulate the wandering Israelites who, focusing on lack, preferred to complain. Your power is awesome; thank You for generously supplying my needs each and every day. Amen.

You open Your hand and satisfy
the desire of every living thing.
PSALM 145:16 NKJV

DAY 59
Abundant Life

I will never have to doubt Your motivation, Lord. You've stated it so clearly in this verse. Your heart for Your children is life—and abundant life, at that. You're not interested in settling for an ordinary, humdrum existence, one day dragging to the next. No, You want to stir us up, to create an adventurous road, to use us in miraculous ways. Wow! You sent Your Son, Jesus, the Life Giver, to show us how to live. May we learn from His example, Father, so that our impact on this world will be a thing of beauty. Amen.

"The thief comes only to steal and kill and destroy. I came that they may have life and have it abundantly."

John 10:10 esv

DAY 60
My Future Is Secure

Every time I fasten my seat belt, I feel secure, Lord. I'm strapped in. Safe. The same is true with my future, now that I've believed in Your Son to save me for all eternity. My spiritual seat belt is fastened tight, but I take absolutely no credit for this. You're holding everything in place. When I come to grips with this truth, I'm assured of something so amazing: I don't have to be scared of tomorrow. I can take bold steps into the unknown. I can see it as an adventure. I'm strapped in tight with You, Father, and You hold the steering wheel. (That fact alone brings the most comfort.) Praise You, Lord. Amen.

God saved you by his grace when you believed. And you can't take credit for this; it is a gift from God.
EPHESIANS 2:8 NLT

DAY 61
The Teacher of All Things

My ability to retain the things I learned in school is limited at best. And, while I'd like to consider myself to be a good student, Lord, I often fall short—even when You're trying to teach me a life lesson. Thank You for sending Your helper, the Holy Spirit. What a blessing, to know that Your plans for my life will all become clearer with His help. You are the teacher of all things, Father, which means that You have high hopes for me! I'm so grateful, Lord. Amen.

"But the Advocate, the Holy Spirit, whom the Father
will send in my name, will teach you all things and
will remind you of everything I have said to you."

JOHN 14:26 NIV

DAY 62
All-Knowing

You know, Lord! Even when I don't, You know *all* things about my journey—which road I should take, which decisions I should make, which plans are established for me. You also know how to speak to my heart and offer guidance every step of the way. You are my all-knowing Father, the only one who truly has my best interest at heart. I settle the issue once and for all, this very day. I trust You to lead me according to Your sovereign will. Amen.

Oh, the depth of the riches both of the wisdom and knowledge of God! How unsearchable are His judgments and His ways past finding out! "For who has known the mind of the LORD? Or who has become His counselor?"

ROMANS 11:33–34 NKJV

DAY 63
You've Shown the Way

I never have to guess with You, Lord. You're a terrific leader. Your Word, the Bible, gives me great guidance. You also lead me as You gently whisper directions in my ear. You nudge me forward with life's circumstances as well. Any time I'm feeling confused, You're right there, showing me the way. Because You've done this so many millions of times before, I know You'll do it again. And all You ask in exchange is that I continue to walk with You, living as You've shown me how to live, loving those You've given me to love. Now that's a good deal, Father! Thank You. Amen.

He has shown you, O man, what is good; and what does the LORD require of you but to do justly, to love mercy, and to walk humbly with your God?

MICAH 6:8 NKJV

DAY 64
Every Good Gift

Father, thank You for the blessings You have poured out on my family. Often I dwell on that which we do not have. Please remind me to be ever grateful for so many gifts. The comforts we enjoy each day like running water and electricity are so easily taken for granted. Thank You for Your provision in our lives. Help me to have a thankful heart so that my family might be more thankful also. Amen.

Thou shalt rejoice in every good thing which the LORD thy God hath given unto thee, and unto thine house, thou, and the Levite, and the stranger that is among you.
DEUTERONOMY 26:11 KJV

DAY 65
Just Do It

Dear Lord, I want to have an obedient heart. Sometimes, when You speak to me, I feel hesitation or want to postpone what You're telling me to do. Yet that means either I don't trust You or I want my own way, neither of which is good. A child ought to obey her parents because she acknowledges their right to direct her and because she trusts the love behind the words. Help me, Lord, to embrace that kind of attitude when You speak to me. In Christ's name, amen.

But be doers of the word, and not hearers only, deceiving yourselves.

JAMES 1:22 NKJV

DAY 66
God Knows Me

God, the Bible says that You knew me even before I was formed in my mother's womb. I find confidence in this. You have been with me all along this journey! As I face this day, help me to remember that I am never alone. You go before me to prepare the future. You walk with me through the present. And You were there with me since before I was born. Wow! Amen.

For thou hast possessed my reins: thou hast covered me in my mother's womb. I will praise thee; for I am fearfully and wonderfully made: marvellous are thy works; and that my soul knoweth right well.

PSALM 139:13–14 KJV

DAY 67
Perfect Peace

I confess, Lord, my thoughts don't remain fixed, or still, very often. They ping-pong from place to place, problem to problem, incident to incident. They soar up and then down again. I'm like a kid on a roller coaster much of the time. One of the hardest challenges I've faced in my walk with You is slowing my mind long enough to actually "stay" on You. But I'm working on it, Father. I love this promise that You will keep my mind in perfect peace once I'm able to come into Your presence and shift my focus to You. As the storms around me calm, my trust grows. Help me with this, Father. I want to be fixed on You. Amen.

"You will keep him in perfect peace, whose mind is stayed on You, because he trusts in You."
ISAIAH 26:3 NKJV

DAY 68
His Purpose Will Stand

You're the reason, Lord. You're the reason I'm still plowing forward. It's Your plans, Your goals, Your energy, Your passion, Your holy calling on my life. I've planned a million things in my life, and few of them came to fruition. I had some degree of passion, but was lacking the "reason." Without a purpose, plans are just plans. I'm discovering Your reason, even now, Father. You want me to reach others with the Gospel message. When I'm moving in that direction, Your purposes stand as straight and tall as arrows. But when I turn my eyes to self, I stumble and fall. Thank You for keeping me aright today, Lord, as I share Your love with all I meet! Amen.

Many are the plans in the mind of a man,
but it is the purpose of the LORD that will stand.
PROVERBS 19:21 ESV

DAY 69
For My Peace

I'm glad that true peace comes from You, Lord, and not from the world around me. People are always telling me how to obtain their version of peace, but it never lasts long. Sometimes I feel so burdened by troubles that it's hard to clear my mind. Then You show up, Father, sweeping away the turmoil in my heart and offering hope that my situation can and will change. My favorite part of this verse is the word *leave*, Lord. You're leaving Your peace with me. It's not on loan—it's mine forever. What a generous God You are! I'm so grateful. Amen.

"Peace I leave with you; my peace I give you.
I do not give to you as the world gives. Do not let
your hearts be troubled and do not be afraid."

JOHN 14:27 NIV

DAY 70
The Mission Field

Father, I believe the mission field You have for me is right here at home, but I know You want me to be involved in world missions as well. Help me to faithfully pray for our missionaries. Give me wisdom as to how You would have me financially support them, and show me any other way I can help them. Amen.

It is more blessed to give than to receive.
ACTS 20:35 KJV

DAY 71
Unlimited Resources

Father, the Bible says You own "the cattle on a thousand hills." You have unlimited resources. So I'm asking You to supply a special need I have today. Although I try to be a good steward of the money You give me, some unexpected event has caught me without the necessary funds. I know You can remedy this situation, if You deem that good for me. Because You're my Father, I'm asking for Your financial advice. I need Your wisdom in this area of my life. Amen.

"For every animal of the forest is mine,
and the cattle on a thousand hills."

PSALM 50:10 NIV

DAY 72
Joyful Regardless of Circumstances

Lord, there are days when I can't help but rejoice in what You are doing. But many times the daily grind is just rather humdrum. There is nothing to rejoice about, much less give thanks for! Or is there? Help me, Father, to be joyful and thankful every day. Each day is a gift from You. Remind me of this truth today, and give me a joyful, thankful heart, I ask. Amen.

Rejoice evermore. Pray without ceasing.
In every thing give thanks: for this is the will
of God in Christ Jesus concerning you.

1 Thessalonians 5:16–18 KJV

DAY 73
What Would Jesus Do?

Heavenly Father, sometimes I am a Sunday Christian. How I want to worship You with the rest of my week! Please help me to be mindful of You throughout the week. May Your will and Your ways permeate my thoughts and decisions. Whether I am taking care of things at home or working with others in the workplace, may I glorify You in all that I say and do. Amen.

*Whether therefore ye eat, or drink,
or whatsoever ye do, do all to the glory of God.*
1 Corinthians 10:31 kjv

DAY 74
Restored

God, I'm grappling with failure. In something in which I wanted so badly to succeed, I've had a less than stellar performance. In fact, humiliating is more like it. I've failed to accomplish my own goals. And I've disappointed others I care about. So where do I go from here? I'm not a quitter, yet I admit I'm lacking motivation to try again. Please give me the courage I need, and help me remember all those Bible characters who refused to be defined by failure, but instead sought grace, attempted the challenge again, and triumphed. Let my story be like theirs, I pray. In Jesus' name, amen.

Restore to me the joy of Your salvation,
and uphold me by Your generous Spirit.
PSALM 51:12 NKJV

DAY 75
Gently Leading

What a gentle leader You are, Father! I've had earthly leaders who left something to be desired. They pushed too hard, asked too much, or insisted on their own way. But You? You're just the opposite, Lord. You're such a gentle and good shepherd. When I'm weary, You lead me beside still waters. When I'm ready to collapse, You point out places along the path where I can rest. Unlike most earthly leaders, You're more interested in me—in my well-being—than anything else. And yet somehow You manage to do it all for Your name's sake. I want to be that kind of leader, Lord. May I learn from Your amazing example. Amen.

The LORD is my shepherd, I lack nothing.
He makes me lie down in green pastures, he leads
me beside quiet waters, he refreshes my soul.
He guides me along the right paths for his name's sake.
PSALM 23:1–3 NIV

DAY 76
Your Eyes Saw

It's so fascinating to think that You knew me even before I was born, Lord. Wow! When I was in my mother's womb, You kept careful watch. Even then, You knew who I would become, where I would live, whose lives I would impact. Thank You for calling me even from before my birth, Father! If my mother could trust You with the intimate details of my birth, surely I can trust You with the plans You have for my life. Amen.

My frame was not hidden from you when I was made in the secret place, when I was woven together in the depths of the earth. Your eyes saw my unformed body; all the days ordained for me were written in your book before one of them came to be.
Psalm 139:15–16 niv

DAY 77
Martha's Trap

Lord, I want to be a servant, but I want it to be done Your way. Please don't let me get caught in Martha's trap of meeting only the physical needs. Although those elements are important, they don't reach the whole person. Let me be a blessing in the spiritual and emotional areas too. Amen.

Give, and it shall be given unto you; good measure, pressed down, and shaken together, and running over, shall men give into your bosom. For with the same measure that ye mete withal it shall be measured to you again.

LUKE 6:38 KJV

DAY 78
Loving My Enemies

Lord, some of Your commands are easy to understand, such as taking care of widows and orphans. But some of them go against human nature. It's easier to show mercy to those we love, but You tell us to love our enemies. You command us to love those who are hard to love. Give me a love for the unlovable, Father. I want to have a heart that pleases You. Amen.

*For if ye love them which love you, what reward
have ye? do not even the publicans the same?
And if ye salute your brethren only, what do ye
more than others? do not even the publicans so?*
MATTHEW 5:46–47 KJV

DAY 79
Every Need Met

Oh, how I love the word *every*, Lord. You don't just want to meet my financial needs. You don't just long to meet my physical needs. You're not going to stop until *every* need is met. What peace this brings! When my needs are emotional, You're there. When I'm in need of provision, You've got it covered. There's not a need I could name that You haven't already provided for. Wow. It boggles my mind when I think about the "everys" in my life. You've got 'em, Lord, and I'm so grateful. Amen.

And my God will meet all your needs according to the riches of his glory in Christ Jesus.
PHILIPPIANS 4:19 NIV

DAY 80
Strengthened with Power

It's a glorious feeling, Father, to wake up feeling so refreshed, so energized, that I could take the world by storm. That's what it's like after spending time in Your presence too. When I take the time to bring my needs and my concerns to You, I leave feeling much better. You pour out Your Spirit, and that amazing supernatural energy of Yours empowers me. I can't drum up this kind of power, Father. It comes only from You. I'm so very grateful for Your strength, Lord! Amen.

For this reason I kneel before the Father, from whom every family in heaven and on earth derives its name. I pray that out of his glorious riches he may strengthen you with power through his Spirit in your inner being.
EPHESIANS 3:14–16 NIV

DAY 81
Live Together with Him

I know what it's like to live in a crowded house, Lord. I've had to share space with others and it's not always comfortable. But sharing space with You? That's a privilege! When I said yes to Your Son, You swept me into Your home and welcomed me to dwell with You. I'm honored to live with You, Father. Thanks for throwing out the welcome mat! Amen.

Since we belong to the day, let us be sober, putting on faith and love as a breastplate, and the hope of salvation as a helmet. For God did not appoint us to suffer wrath but to receive salvation through our Lord Jesus Christ. He died for us so that, whether we are awake or asleep, we may live together with him.

1 Thessalonians 5:8–10 niv

DAY 82
Twinkle, Twinkle

Lord, You don't just know the number of stars, You actually *determine* the number of stars. You decide where to place them, how big they should be—everything. And You care enough about each one that You take the time to give them names. I'm looking forward to hearing these names when I get to heaven. What fun that will be! You're definitely in the details, Father. Nothing slips by You. To say You care about the little things would be an understatement. If You care about them, I can only imagine how You must feel about us, Your kids. You've called us by name too, and called us to shine just like those stars above. Today, may I shimmer as never before. Thanks for caring so much, Lord. Amen.

He determines the number of the stars
and calls them each by name.

PSALM 147:4 NIV

DAY 83
Bless His Name

Jesus, You alone are worthy of all of my praise. I bless Your name. One day I will worship You with no end, no holding back, and no earthly distraction. I will worship You in heaven forever and ever. . .with the angels and with all of Your people. For today, I go into Your world and I will choose to bless Your name in the present. Accept my offering of praise. Amen.

And I beheld, and I heard the voice of many angels round about the throne and the beasts and the elders: and the number of them was ten thousand times ten thousand, and thousands of thousands; saying with a loud voice, Worthy is the Lamb that was slain to receive power, and riches, and wisdom, and strength, and honour, and glory, and blessing.
REVELATION 5:11–12 KJV

DAY 84
Provision for Missions

In Your Word, You've commanded us to take the Gospel to all nations. You've also said that when we're obedient, You'll meet our needs. Please meet the needs of our missionaries, Lord. Provide what they need physically and spiritually, and let many souls be saved as a result. In Jesus' name, amen.

Therefore take no thought, saying, What shall we eat? or, What shall we drink? or, Wherewithal shall we be clothed?... for your heavenly Father knoweth that ye have need of all these things.
MATTHEW 6:31–32 KJV

DAY 85
Buoyancy of Faith

God, I've seen swollen rivers; I've watched raging water destroy entire communities. And right now, I feel like the tide of my life is reaching flood level. I'm struggling to keep my head above water, but the waves keep crashing over me. This struggle with depression is almost more than I can bear. Sometimes I just want to surrender to the current and slip under the water. But others are depending on me, and You would be hurt if I chose to end this journey that way. Please hold me up in this flood; Your hands are the only ones that can. Amen.

"When you pass through the waters, I will be with you; and through the rivers, they shall not overflow you."

Isaiah 43:2 NKJV

DAY 86
A Proper Outlook

So often, Lord, I see relationships crumbling, and much of the time a money issue is what starts the process. Some people are careless or dishonest in their spending; others just want too much. As a result there is a lot of bitterness and hatred. Please help me to have a proper outlook when money is involved. In Jesus' name, amen.

He that loveth silver shall not be satisfied
with silver; nor he that loveth abundance
with increase: this is also vanity.
ECCLESIASTES 5:10 KJV

DAY 87
One Step, Two Step

I haven't counted my steps since I was a child, Lord. I remember doing it, though, to gauge distance. Of course, my tiny strides were a far cry from the steps I take today. It's fascinating to realize something as small as a step is on Your mind. You have so many other things to keep up with, Father! But there You are, watching me go here and there and keeping track of every step I take. May every move I make bring me closer to You, Lord. I don't want to waste even one step. I want every last one to count and to make a difference for Your kingdom. Use me, Lord, I pray. Amen.

"Does he not see my ways
and count my every step?"

Job 31:4 NIV

DAY 88
Superglue

Father, You're like cosmic superglue. You hold all things together. When I make plans, they often crumble. I set off on the right path, and before long things come unraveled. With You behind the wheel, things stick together. The plan works out. No unraveling. No crumbling. That's because You've got the power to hold things steady, even when everything around me is shaking. Have I mentioned how grateful I am for that? Praise You, Lord! I'll stick with You as You stick with the plan. Amen.

He is before all things, and in
him all things hold together.
Colossians 1:17 esv

DAY 89
Like-Minded with My Father

I don't always know or understand Your thoughts, Lord; but I am created in Your image, which gives me glimpses into Your will for my life. Thank You for giving me the mind of Christ. What a privilege, to be like-minded with You, Lord! May my heart beat in sync with Yours and may my thought life respond as You guide my every step. Amen.

Then God said, "Let us make human beings in our image, to be like us. They will reign over the fish in the sea, the birds in the sky, the livestock, all the wild animals on the earth, and the small animals that scurry along the ground."

GENESIS 1:26 NLT

DAY 90
Good-Gift Giver

You give great gifts, Father. Walking with You is like Christmas 365 days a year. Your gifts are more fun to unwrap and last longer than any I've been given. I won't be returning any of them either! They're hand-tailored, just for me. You know best how to deliver them and how to teach me to use them. If I have any problems, I go straight to the owner's manual (Your Word) for direction. Oh, how I've loved discovering all of these gifts, Lord. Thank You for entrusting them to me. I promise to use them for You. Amen.

"Which of you, if your son asks for bread, will give him a stone? Or if he asks for a fish, will give him a snake? If you, then, though you are evil, know how to give good gifts to your children, how much more will your Father in heaven give good gifts to those who ask him!"

MATTHEW 7:9–11 NIV

DAY 91
Extras

Dear God, I am so thankful that You have provided for me. Sometimes that blessing even goes above and beyond my needs. I now ask for wisdom in handling these gifts. My desire is to glorify You and to make sure that I'm not controlled by money. Please help me use it in a way that honors You. Amen.

My God shall supply all your need according to his riches in glory by Christ Jesus.
PHILIPPIANS 4:19 KJV

DAY 92
My Pastor

Thank You for my pastor, dear God. He loves You; and he loves those to whom he ministers. Knowing that his desire is to present the truths of the Bible is a great comfort in a world that is full of false teachings. Bless my pastor as he continues to preach Your Word. In Jesus' name, amen.

*And he gave some, apostles; and some, prophets;
and some, evangelists; and some, pastors and teachers;
for the perfecting of the saints, for the work of the
ministry, for the edifying of the body of Christ.*
EPHESIANS 4:11–12 KJV

DAY 93
Joy in God's Word

Thank You, God, that in Your holy scriptures I find the ways of life. I find wise counsel in the pages of my Bible. You reveal the truth to me, Lord, and there is no greater blessing than to know the truth. You tell me in Your Word that the truth sets me free. I am free to live a life that brings You glory and honor. May others see the joy I have found in You! Amen.

Thou hast made known to me the ways of life;
thou shalt make me full of joy with thy countenance.
ACTS 2:28 KJV

DAY 94
The Power of Words

Father, my mouth sometimes gets me into trouble. Please keep me aware of the things I say that aren't right. Let me back up and apologize if I've hurt anyone. Better yet, let me consider my words before I cast them out on the wind. Once spoken, they can never be recalled. Your written Word is living, brilliant, and powerful; Jesus is the embodiment of it—the Living Word. My spoken earthly words are weighty as well; they can minister life or death to those who hear. I ask You to remind me of this throughout the day. Amen.

Death and life are in the power of the tongue:
and they that love it shall eat the fruit thereof.
PROVERBS 18:21 KJV

DAY 95
You Say I Can Overcome

I don't always feel like an overcomer, Lord. So many times I just want to crawl into a hole and hide away, to give up completely. But You won't let me! You just keep saying, "You can do this, girl," followed by, "Trust Me" and, "Let Me lead you every step of the way." I'm listening to those words of encouragement today, Father. I really need them. You're an overcomer, and I'm created in Your image, which means I'm an overcomer too. I'll stand in that knowledge today, Lord. Amen.

"I have told you all this so that you may have peace in me.
Here on earth you will have many trials and sorrows.
But take heart, because I have overcome the world."

JOHN 16:33 NLT

DAY 96
You Say I Can Shine Like a Star

I must confess: Sometimes my candle feels more like a dying ember than a shining star, Lord. I reach the burnt-out stage pretty quickly. Even on the best of days, I don't always shine like I should. Thank You for the reminder that You've called me to shine like the brightness of the firmament. I can only do this if I'm a reflection of You, and that's my chief aim from this moment on. It's not my glory, Father. It's not my light. It's all You, Lord. May I be a beautiful reflection of You. Amen.

"Those who are wise will shine like the brightness of the heavens, and those who lead many to righteousness, like the stars for ever and ever."

DANIEL 12:3 NIV

DAY 97
Your Unfailing Love

How many times have I slipped on proverbial banana peels, Lord? Dozens! I'm walking along just fine, and then down I go. It brings great comfort to know You catch me when I fall. You're the King of soft landings! You're there for me because You love me. (This I have experienced and know to be true.) Even in my deepest troubles, You've held me upright and put a smile on my face. Father, You must have big plans for me. You've kept me upright so that I can keep moving forward with You. Praise You for Your great love. Amen.

When I said, "My foot is slipping," your unfailing love, LORD, supported me. When anxiety was great within me, your consolation brought me joy.
PSALM 94:18–19 NIV

DAY 98
You Speak with Authority

All authority. All. What an amazing and bold declaration, Lord! There is no one besides You. No one to ask. No one to approach. No one to beg. You are the be-all and end-all, Father, and Your words (both over my life and over this universe) carry weight. With You, Lord, I can say, "The buck stops here," and mean it. "Whom have I in heaven but you?" (Psalm 73:25 NIV). No one, Father! You are enough. I submit myself to Your holy authority and bend my ear toward heaven, ready to hear Your responses to all of life's questions. Amen.

Then Jesus came to them and said, "All authority in heaven and on earth has been given to me."
MATTHEW 28:18 NIV

DAY 99
Golden Words Needed

Heavenly Father, today I need affirming words. You know that words are important to me as a woman. You also know that I struggle with self-worth. The other people in my world don't always meet my need to be affirmed verbally, and I can't expect them to fulfill every void in my life. So, Lord, let me look to and in Your Word to find the love and encouragement I need. In Jesus' name, amen.

A word fitly spoken is like apples of gold in settings of silver.
PROVERBS 25:11 NKJV

DAY 100
Never Give Up

Lord, I don't want to be a quitter; but I've tried so hard to be like You, and I keep messing up. I know You said that with You all things are possible, and I need to be reminded of that daily. Don't let me give up. Help me to remember that You aren't finished with me yet. Amen.

Wherefore, my beloved, as ye have always obeyed, not as in my presence only, but now much more in my absence, work out your own salvation with fear and trembling. For it is God which worketh in you both to will and to do of his good pleasure.
PHILIPPIANS 2:12–13 KJV

DAY 101
Fitness

It's an exercise-crazy world we live in, Lord. Gym membership are prized, morning jogs are eulogized, and workout clothing has become a fashion statement. There are some who make this area of self-care too important; they spend an inordinate amount of time on it. Yet others don't keep it high enough on their priority list. Help me, God, to keep the proper perspective of fitness, because, after all, I have a responsibility for the upkeep on this body. It's on loan from You. Amen.

Physical training is of some value, but godliness has value for all things, holding promise for both the present life and the life to come.

1 TIMOTHY 4:8 NIV

DAY 102
The One Who Is

Heavenly Father, today I'm grateful for all You are—the God who is, the God of the living, the great I Am. Your character is unchanging. You are the epitome of perfect holiness and love. Because of who and all You are, I believe and trust in You. Your truthfulness is indisputable and Your power is established. Not just for the majestic works by Your hand but for the pure glory of Your nature—I worship You today. Amen.

Who is like the Lord our God,
who dwells on high?
Psalm 113:5 nkjv

DAY 103
A Giving Heart

Father, may I be honest? Sometimes I don't feel like serving. They keep asking if I will help with this or that at church. And there is always a collection being taken up. Can't I just focus on me? I have my own needs! But oh, the peace I feel when I lay my head on my pillow at night knowing I have loved with action, with sacrifice. Make me a giver, I ask. Amen.

Remember the words of the Lord Jesus, how he said,
It is more blessed to give than to receive.
ACTS 20:35 KJV

DAY 104
Coveting

God, it's so easy to break the tenth commandment: Do not covet (see Exodus 20:17). Coveting is a way of life for many in our world. But You say we shouldn't compare ourselves with the "Joneses," nor envy them and what they have. Whatever You've given me is to be enjoyed and received, not held up for inspection. Teach me a deeper gratefulness for Your blessings. In Jesus' name, amen.

Let your conduct be without covetousness.

HEBREWS 13:5 NKJV

DAY 105
Divine Guidance

Dear Lord, it's so hard sometimes to know what Your will is. You don't write specific instructions in the sky nor emblazon them on a marquee. So how can I know exactly what You want me to do? How can I keep from making a big mistake? How can I proceed with this decision? I ask today that You would give me wisdom; please send me guidance as I seek Your will. Through a person, a thought, a scripture, let me sense Your leading for this situation. I want my life to honor Your plan for me. In Christ's name, amen.

If any of you lacks wisdom, you should ask God,
who gives generously to all without finding
fault, and it will be given to you.

JAMES 1:5 NIV

DAY 106
A God-Centered Home

Father, so many homes are shaken in these days. So many families are shattering to pieces around me. Protect my home, I pray. Protect my loved ones. Be the foundation of my home, strong and solid, consistent and wise. May every decision made here reflect Your principles. May those who visit this home and encounter this family be keenly aware of our uniqueness, because we serve the one true and almighty God. Amen.

Except the LORD build the house, they labour in vain that build it: except the LORD keep the city, the watchman waketh but in vain.

PSALM 127:1 KJV

DAY 107
God's Book of Wisdom

There are so many "how-to" books available today, Lord, and they all promise to increase my knowledge in some area. But not one of them gives any hope for added wisdom. Only Your Word offers that. Thank You for providing the means to know You more fully and to live life more abundantly. Amen.

For the word of the LORD is right;
and all his works are done in truth.

PSALM 33:4 KJV

DAY 108
Love Covers Sins

Lord, all of my sin was nailed to the cross when Your Son died for me. Without grace, I am but filthy rags before a holy God. But through Christ, I am adopted as Your daughter, forgiven. There is pride in this daughter, God. Pride that resists forgiveness. Pride that says "I am right." Remind me of the multitude of my own sins that Your love covered through Jesus. Help me to love others well. Amen.

Hatred stirreth up strifes:
but love covereth all sins.
PROVERBS 10:12 KJV

DAY 109
A Generous Supply

God, there is no creature on earth You do not see or provide for. I'm bringing praise to You right now for the daily things You supply for me. It is through Your goodness that I have food to eat, clothes to wear, and water to drink. Help me always be thankful for what I have and not emulate the wandering Israelites who, focusing on lack, preferred to complain. Your power is awesome; thank You for generously supplying my needs each and every day. Amen.

You open Your hand and satisfy the
desire of every living thing.
PSALM 145:16 NKJV

DAY 110
That Important First Step

Lord, my neighbors are some of the most rude and inconsiderate people I've ever known. It's hard not to complain about them, but I don't have a right to. They aren't Christians, and I've never witnessed to them. Why would they act differently? Forgive me, Father. I will take them Your Word. Please open their hearts. Amen.

Walk in wisdom toward them that
are without, redeeming the time.
Colossians 4:5 kjv

DAY 111
One Nation Under God

Dear God, I am so weary of the bickering in our nation. It disturbs me to see people attempting to remove You from schools, courtrooms, and anywhere else they think of. They distort history and deny that this nation was founded with You as her leader. Heal us, Lord. Help us return to You! Amen.

I am the light of the world: he that followeth me shall not walk in darkness, but shall have the light of life.

JOHN 8:12 KJV

DAY 112
Don't Worry!

Dear Lord, Your Word tells me it is wrong to worry. I try to tell myself that it's only concern, but actually, that's putting a nice spin on the issue. Older women used to say that females are just born worriers. I guess there's some truth to that, maybe because we're so invested in relationships, and most of our worrying is about those we love and care for. Still, You know worry isn't good for us and it doesn't accomplish anything. So, today, help me not to worry, but to turn all my "concerns" over to You. Amen.

Do not be anxious about anything, but in every situation, by prayer and petition, with thanksgiving, present your requests to God. And the peace of God, which transcends all understanding, will guard your hearts and your minds in Christ Jesus.
PHILIPPIANS 4:6–7 NIV

DAY 113
Think on Pure Things

There's just not much in today's society that encourages purity, but Your Word certainly demonstrates the importance of focusing our attention upon things that are pure. From experience, I have learned that life is more satisfying when it's geared toward pleasing You rather than the flesh, and I thank You for these lessons. Amen.

Ye shall walk after the LORD your God, and fear him, and keep his commandments, and obey his voice, and ye shall serve him, and cleave unto him.

DEUTERONOMY 13:4 KJV

DAY 114
Help with Priorities

Dear God, I need help with my priorities. It is so easy for them to get out of whack. Show me the things I've let creep to the top that don't belong there. Point out to me those areas where I need to put more emphasis and commitment. Lord, let me remember that people are worth more than possessions and pursuits. Let my unseen checklist of priorities reflect that. Amen.

"For where your treasure is,
there your heart will be also."
Matthew 6:21 niv

DAY 115
Today!

Father in heaven, I have a tendency to try to live a week or month at a time. It's difficult for me to limit myself to one day, one hour, one minute. But that's how You want me to live. You know that projecting into the future causes me to wonder and worry about things that haven't happened yet. You also know that I can't be any good to anyone if my head is in the clouds, thinking about the future. So help me live in today—it's all I have at the moment. Amen.

"Does He not see my ways,
and count all my steps?"
JOB 31:4 NKJV

DAY 116
When I'm Not Prepared

Father God, I've put myself in a bind because I procrastinated. I knew this was looming ahead of me, but I wanted to do other things first. Or, at least, I wanted to leave the task until the right time. But now, there is no more time, and I'm not prepared. Please help me, Lord, working all things to my good. Amen.

Make the most of every opportunity.
EPHESIANS 5:16 NLT

Jesus, like the good Samaritan in Your parable, may I too show mercy. Some may never enter the doors of a church, but what a difference an act of grace could make! Put before me opportunities to show unmerited favor. That is, after all, what You have shown to me. You died for my sins. I never could have earned salvation. It is a free gift, an act of grace. Make me merciful. Amen.

Which now of these three, thinkest thou, was neighbour unto him that fell among the thieves? And he said, He that shewed mercy on him. Then said Jesus unto him, Go, and do thou likewise.

LUKE 10:36–37 KJV

DAY 118
From the Mountain

Lord, it feels good to be alive! When I got out of bed this morning, I had this wonderful sense of well-being. Some days I awaken with something negative on my mind, some trouble on the horizon, or some ache in my body. But today I feel great in mind, spirit, and body. This road of life has both mountains and valleys. But right now, I'm going to enjoy the mountain—the brightness, the beauty, and the refreshing that will help me face any challenge that comes my way today or tomorrow. I love You, Lord. Thank You for good surprises! Amen.

Oh, give thanks to the LORD, for He is good!
For His mercy endures forever.
PSALM 107:1 NKJV

DAY 119
You Look at My Heart

Lord, it troubles me to see how much interest people put in outward appearance. Clothing. Shoes. Makeup. Hairstyles. These things are fine, but when they become the focus—the primary things people notice—something is amiss. I'm so glad You're not examining me from the outside in, making sure I measure up to society's standards. Thank You for looking at my heart. Not that my heart is perfect, as You well know, but You're so good at ironing out the wrinkles when things are off-kilter internally. What a gracious God You are. Amen.

But the LORD said to Samuel, "Do not consider his appearance or his height, for I have rejected him. The LORD does not look at the things people look at. People look at the outward appearance, but the LORD looks at the heart."

1 SAMUEL 16:7 NIV

DAY 120
An Enlightened Heart

What a lovely image, Lord! I can have an enlightened heart, one flooded with light. Wow. When the light is turned on, my vision is amplified. I'm able to see the future as a positive place, no matter what I'm going through today. And what an awesome reminder that You've prepared an inheritance for me—a rich and glorious one, at that. May the eyes of my heart be completely enlightened so that I never forget You are for me, not against me. Praise You, Father. Amen.

I pray that your hearts will be flooded with light so that you can understand the confident hope he has given to those he called—his holy people who are his rich and glorious inheritance.

EPHESIANS 1:18 NLT

DAY 121
I Place My Hope in You

Sometimes it's hard to see past the fog. So many dismal things happen in a row and they cloud my vision. But I love the images this verse presents, Lord. When my face is to the ground, when I feel like my heart is twisted in a thousand directions, You long to renew my hope. That's when I need it most, Father! It begins with praise, so I choose to do that today. I won't gaze with fear at the circumstances. Instead, I deliberately choose to lift my eyes toward You, that my hope may be restored. Amen.

Why are you cast down, O my soul, and why are you in turmoil within me? Hope in God; for I shall again praise him, my salvation and my God.

PSALM 43:5 ESV

DAY 122
Rejoice in Hope

Patience. You had to go there, didn't You, Lord? We both know that patience isn't my strong suit! But I'm working on it, Father. When troubles come, I tend to panic, not pray. But today I turn my voice, my woes, my concerns to You. Instead of whining, I choose to praise. I'll rejoice in the fact that You've got this. You're standing right next to me, ready to offer hope. So, instead of running, I'll stand firm. I'll be patient, difficult as that might be. I'll keep on knocking on the doors of heaven and standing firm in the hope You've given me. Thank You, Lord. Amen.

Rejoice in our confident hope.
Be patient in trouble, and keep on praying.
Romans 12:12 NLT

DAY 123
Written on Their Hearts

I get overwhelmed when I think of how personal Your plans for my life are, God. The covenants that You've made with me are, in many ways, like the laws You wrote on the hearts of Your people in Old Testament times. When You take the time to write something on my heart, I know You mean it. You won't go back on Your word. We're talking about a permanent etching here, one that sticks. I'm completely humbled to think You would care enough about me to write something so personal, just for me. Bless You, Father! Amen.

"This is the covenant I will make with the people of Israel after that time," declares the LORD. "I will put my law in their minds and write it on their hearts. I will be their God, and they will be my people."

JEREMIAH 31:33 NIV

DAY 124
Be Still

I'm so busy, Lord! There are days when I'm rushing here and there and barely pause to catch my breath. On those days, I often forget to meet with You. Sometimes, in the craziness, I also forget that You've already made plans for me. I strike out on my own without asking Your opinion. Thank You for the reminder that pausing to be with You is the first step to a great day. Teach me to be still in Your presence, to wait on You. I'll need a lot of reminding, Lord, but don't give up on me. What a blessing to know that You will fight for me, if I will only slow down long enough to let You. Amen.

"The LORD will fight for you;
you need only to be still."
EXODUS 14:14 NIV

DAY 125
Your Words Are Exalted

Lord, Your Word is exalted above all. Even a decree from the greatest ruler on earth can't compare. The opinions of Hollywood stars don't even come close. Even the finest teachers and educators can't speak with the same level of authority that You have. Thank You for the reminder that all I have to do is be still and know that You are God. When I'm in that position of submission, You are exalted in all the earth. Oh, what a magnificent Father You are. Be exalted forever, Lord! Amen.

He says, "Be still, and know that I am God;
I will be exalted among the nations,
I will be exalted in the earth."
PSALM 46:10 NIV

All Things Are Possible

I've pondered this verse long and hard, Lord. It's remarkable to think that *all* things are possible if only I believe. I know, of course, that *all* refers to the things that are inside of Your will and Your plan for my life. But how remarkable to know that I play a role in seeing these things come to pass. There's power in believing. Today I choose to believe that Your plans for my life are good. I choose to believe that I have a hopeful future. If ever I doubt, Father, remind me afresh that all I have to do is believe. Amen.

Jesus said to him, "'If You can'! All things are possible for one who believes."

MARK 9:23 ESV

DAY 127
Acquainted with All My Ways

I often use the phrase "No one knows me like I know myself," but that's not true, Lord. You know me better than I know myself. You know every detail—my likes, my dislikes, my hopes, my dreams, my disappointments, my joys. You're acquainted not only with the things I've done in the past but also with what I hope to accomplish in the future. Because You know me from the inside out, I am confident in Your ability to scrutinize my path and make a way for me. It's exciting to see where You will take me next, Lord. Amen.

You know when I sit and when I rise; you perceive my thoughts from afar. You discern my going out and my lying down; you are familiar with all my ways.

PSALM 139:2–3 NIV

DAY 128

Perseverance

Lord, I so often reach the point of giving up when I'm following my own path. Somehow, knowing You're the one with the plan gives me the wherewithal to keep going. I'll persevere, Father, because I know You're ultimately the one in charge. I submit myself to Your will and Your process, Lord. It's not always easy, but I will do my best to put one foot in front of the other as I walk out this remarkable plan You've set in motion for my life. Amen.

*You need to persevere so that when you
have done the will of God, you will
receive what he has promised.*
HEBREWS 10:36 NIV

DAY 129
Engraved on Your Palms

Lord, You care so deeply for me. I am in wonder and awe as I think about the fact that Your plans for my life are engraved on Your hands. Oh, those wonderful, perfect hands! They lead me, they guide me, they lift me up when I fall. And what an amazing thought, to know that You care enough about me to carry a permanent marking of love. How can I praise You for caring so deeply for me, Father? I stand amazed. Amen.

"See, I have engraved you on the palms of my hands; your walls are ever before me."
ISAIAH 49:16 NIV

DAY 130
He Guides Me Along

Father, what a good trailblazer You are! You guide me along all of the right paths, the ones You've chosen just for me. I acknowledge that Your plans are better than my own. I can set my foot on a path, but if it's not the one You designed for me, then it will get me nowhere. So, I don't just trust in Your guidance, Father, but in the plan too. I can imagine You've got great heavenly blueprints with my name all over them. I submit to the building process, Lord. Amen.

He lets me rest in green pastures. He leads me to calm water. He gives me new strength. He leads me on paths that are right for the good of his name.

PSALM 23:2–3 NCV

DAY 131
Revealed through the Spirit

Sometimes I forget, Lord. I forget that revelation only comes through You. I want to obtain answers—direction—in the usual ways: from friends, loved ones, acquaintances. Even from my own knowledge, obtained from years of walking this planet. Advice is good. Knowledge is good. But I need to hear Your thoughts. Learning to quiet myself and listen to that still, small voice isn't my first inclination, Father. Thank You for the reminder that You've got answers to whisper in my ear, things yet to be revealed. Amen.

These are the things God has revealed to us by his Spirit. The Spirit searches all things, even the deep things of God. For who knows a person's thoughts except their own spirit within them? In the same way no one knows the thoughts of God except the Spirit of God.
1 Corinthians 2:10–11 niv

· DAY 132
Perfect Vision

My vision isn't always the best, Lord. I can see only with my physical eyes most of the time. There's so much more to see when the veil is pulled back. What's going on up there in the heavenly realms? I can only imagine all of the amazing things You're planning, even now. I get so excited when I think about Your goodness, Your heart for me. Even now, Your Spirit is searching deep places, putting the pieces of the puzzle in place. Oh, to have Your heavenly vision, Lord! Can I have a little glimpse? Please? Amen.

But, as it is written, "What no eye has seen, nor ear heard, nor the heart of man imagined, what God has prepared for those who love him"—these things God has revealed to us through the Spirit. For the Spirit searches everything, even the depths of God.
1 CORINTHIANS 2:9–10 ESV

DAY 133

New Compassions

I really didn't want to get up this morning, Father. My blankets seemed like good protection from the cares of the day. But when I saw the glorious sunrise and heard the cheerful, singing birds, I was reminded that Your compassions are new every morning. I knew everything would be fine. Thank You for Your faithfulness. In Jesus' name, amen.

Sing unto the LORD, bless his name;
shew forth his salvation from day to day.

PSALM 96:2 KJV

DAY 134
Gentle Peace

Thank You, Lord, for this opportunity to bask in the peace that You offer. As I sit here in the woods, listening to the creek gently bubbling over the stones, I am reminded how Your presence in my life soothes even in the midst of chaos. I'm glad I have Your peace! Amen.

The LORD bless thee, and keep thee: the LORD make his face shine upon thee, and be gracious unto thee: the LORD lift up his countenance upon thee, and give thee peace.

NUMBERS 6:24–26 KJV

DAY 135
Technology

Dear God, the internet is a marvelous tool! Thank You for giving humankind the ability to invent it. But the internet also has a great potential for evil. I ask You to protect my family from online predators, from sexual content, from sites that would have a negative influence on our relationship with You. Help me to be prudent in my use of the web. Like any other means of communication, it can be used wrongly. But, with Your help, it can be an instrument for good in our home. Amen.

I will set nothing wicked before my eyes.
PSALM 101:3 NKJV

DAY 136
Peace, Please

Dear Jesus, someone I love dearly is in the hospital. I'm sitting here in the busy waiting room, watching for the doctor, wanting news, and yet dreading to hear it. Others surround me, connected to this place by a person they care about. We're people from every stratum and season of life with one thing in common—knowing someone who is suffering physically. Lord, illness and injury have to obey Your will, and so do the emotions that burden the hearts of those here. Please visit every waiting area and patient's room, and bring the cure that only comes from You—tranquility, mercy, and courage. Amen.

Now the God of peace be with you all.
ROMANS 15:33 NKJV

DAY 137
Only One Master

Father, there are so many things in this world that fight for my affection. It seems there is always a new product or style that the advertisements say I can't live without! It is easy to get caught up in materialism. Guard my heart, Father, and guard even my tongue. Remind me that the word *love* should not be used loosely. I love You, Father. Be Lord of my life, I pray. Amen.

No man can serve two masters: for either he will hate the one, and love the other; or else he will hold to the one, and despise the other. Ye cannot serve God and mammon.

MATTHEW 6:24 KJV

DAY 138
A Sense of Purpose

Father, I'm in a rut. I like some familiarity, but this monotony is wearing away at my sense of purpose. I know there are parts of our lives that are not particularly glamorous, fulfilling, or significant (at least, on the surface). Yet living without passion or purpose isn't what You had in mind for us. Show me, Lord, how to find meaning in my everyday life. Open my eyes up to the subtle nuances of joy folded into life's mundane hours. I put my longings into Your hands. Amen.

In Him also we have obtained an inheritance,
being predestined according to the purpose of Him
who works all things according to the counsel of His will.
EPHESIANS 1:11 NKJV

DAY 139
Perfect Holiness

God, when I consider my own inadequacies, I am amazed at Your perfectness. You are truth and justice, holiness and integrity. There is none like You. You are the one and only true God. Other deities disappoint their followers; other idols fail. But You never do. Because You are perfect holiness, all Your other attributes are only good. There is no selfishness, vengefulness, or deceitfulness in You, Lord. Thus, I can trust You completely and revel in Your light unafraid. Amen.

"No one is holy like the LORD, for there is none besides You, nor is there any rock like our God."

1 SAMUEL 2:2 NKJV

DAY 140
Those Left Behind

Father, I'd like to take just a moment to pray for the extended families of missionaries. We often forget that as obedient servants take Your Gospel abroad, their relatives are left behind. The separation can be difficult. Ease the loneliness. Bless each family member in a special way. Amen.

For none of us liveth to himself,
and no man dieth to himself.
ROMANS 14:7 KJV

DAY 141
The Best Relationship

Dear Jesus, I've known many people in my life. I've enjoyed many good relationships and tried to avoid the bad. One thing is certain though. My relationship with You is the most important. I'm so glad You have time for me and that You want me to fellowship with You. I couldn't ask for a better friend. Amen.

*The LORD thy God in the midst of thee is mighty;
he will save, he will rejoice over thee with joy; he will
rest in his love, he will joy over thee with singing.*
ZEPHANIAH 3:17 KJV

DAY 142
A Light on My Path

I know what it's like to stumble around in the dark, Lord. Toes get stubbed. Knees get bumped. Things get knocked over. Sure, my eyes adjust to a certain extent, but I'm still second-guessing myself because things aren't as clear as they should be. I can't make out the road signs. But You provide a light, Father. When I'm feeling unsure, I ask You to brighten my path so that I don't cause damage as I move along. I'm glad You illuminate the road for me, Lord. I praise You for that. Amen.

Your word is a lamp for my feet,
a light on my path.
PSALM 119:105 NIV

DAY 143
Yet to Be Revealed

My vision is so cloudy at times, Lord. I can't see what's coming around the next bend, let alone where You're taking me in this coming season of my life. (Oh, how I wish I could!) Trusting You when I can't see is a bit like walking on water. I don't always have the security of knowing that my eyes won't deceive me, and sometimes I feel like I'm going under. But I know I can trust You, Father. You haven't let me drown yet. I'll keep my eyes on You, Lord. Amen.

Dear friends, now we are children of God, and what we will be has not yet been made known. But we know that when Christ appears, we shall be like him, for we shall see him as he is.

1 John 3:2 niv

DAY 144
Perfectly Knitted

When I ponder the fact that Your work in my life began even before You knit me together in my mother's womb, I'm floored, Father. You thought this out, long before I came into being. You went to so much trouble just to make me who I am. You know everything about, well, *everything*—and that brings such comfort. I know I can trust You, my Creator, to guide me every step of the way. Amen.

You have searched me, LORD, and you know me. You know when I sit and when I rise; you perceive my thoughts from afar. You discern my going out and my lying down; you are familiar with all my ways. . . . Such knowledge is too wonderful for me, too lofty for me to attain.

PSALM 139:1–3, 6 NIV

DAY 145
No Hiding

All things are visible to You, Father. Your kids don't get away with shenanigans because You're an all-seeing God. We are like babes on the changing table, naked and bare before You. There's not a thing about us You don't know: our angst, bitterness, concerns, joys. But You don't leave us to wallow in our woes, Father. (Thank goodness!) Just as a mother changes her child, You are ready to step in and change our hearts. Praise You for seeking us out, Lord. Amen.

Neither is there any creature that is not manifest in his sight: but all things are naked and opened unto the eyes of him with whom we have to do.

HEBREWS 4:13 KJV

DAY 146

You Tell Me to Ask, Seek, Knock

You ask me to take action, Father. You want me to ask, so I come to You boldly, my request made known. You ask me to seek, so, Lord, I seek Your will—and Your way—with my whole heart. Not my will, but Yours, be done, Father. You ask me to knock, so here I stand, Lord, my knuckles rap-rap-rapping on the door of Your heart. I'm engaged in the process and will hover close, asking, seeking, knocking as long as it takes. I'm so grateful for the open doors You are placing in front of me, even now. Amen.

"So I say to you: Ask and it will be given to you; seek and you will find; knock and the door will be opened to you."

LUKE 11:9 NIV

DAY 147
Long Life

I love this promise, Lord! Thank You for this declaration. If I honor my father and mother (and the other elders You've placed in my life), my days will be long. Show me how to respect those You've placed in authority over me. May Your plans for our relationship shine through, even during the tough seasons. And, Father, show me how to lead those You've entrusted to my care (my children or others I teach and tend to). I want them to know the blessing of a good, long life too. May we all, as Your children, learn from You. You're the ultimate Father, and we live to bring honor and glory to Your name. Amen.

"Honor your father and your mother,
so that you may live long in the land
the LORD your God is giving you."
EXODUS 20:12 NIV

DAY 148
I Declare!

Lord, Your declarations are powerful. But You're teaching me that mine can be powerful too. Today, I openly declare that Jesus Christ is Lord. I choose to believe that You raised Him from the dead, Father. Because I truly believe what I'm declaring, I know that I'm made right with You. What an amazing declaration. It has truly changed my life—and my eternity. All praise to You! Amen.

If you openly declare that Jesus is Lord and believe in your heart that God raised him from the dead, you will be saved. For it is by believing in your heart that you are made right with God, and it is by openly declaring your faith that you are saved.

ROMANS 10:9–10 NLT

DAY 149
A Very Full Cup

I know the age-old question, Lord: Do you see the glass as half empty or half full? My answer to this question determines how I view the situations I face. Oh, how I love the idea that Your plans to prosper me include a cup that's overflowing with blessings. I won't be looking for it at the bank, Father, but rather in the tiniest details of my life. You have blessed me with friends, mentors, a job, health, and so many other things. You meet my every need, Father. I am well taken care of. Thank You for filling my cup to the top, Lord. Amen.

Lord, you alone are my inheritance,
my cup of blessing.
PSALM 16:5 NLT

The Oil of Blessing

I get it, Lord. One of the ways You want to prosper me is to teach me to walk in harmony with others. When I choose to live this way, the benefits are as precious as fine oil. (I can almost smell it now!) It's not always easy to get along with folks (even inside the walls of my local church), but I love the idea that our unity causes a sweet-smelling fragrance that others will witness and want for themselves. I'm so grateful for Your oil of blessing, Father. Thank You for showing me how to bring honor to Your name through my relationships. Amen.

For harmony is as precious as the anointing oil that was poured over Aaron's head, that ran down his beard and onto the border of his robe.
PSALM 133:2 NLT

DAY 151
Train Up a Child

Oh Lord, of all Your many declarations, this is one of my favorites! It brings such peace to hear that my children will (eventually) walk the right path. There are days when I wonder, Father. Some have turned to their own way, bringing this scripture into question in my mind. Oh, but how wonderful to realize that "when they are older" (which could be any time now, since we're all aging rapidly), they will not leave it. I'm hanging on to that promise, Father. Amen.

Direct your children onto the right path,
and when they are older, they will not leave it.

PROVERBS 22:6 NLT

DAY 152
All I Need

Heavenly Father, You are a God of hope, joy, and great love. I don't need signs or wonders. I often wait for people or situations to turn from hopeless to hopeful. But my hope is in You. I need not wait for anything else or look for some other source. I quiet myself before You this morning and ask that You renew the hope within my heart. Thank You, Father. Amen.

And now, Lord, what wait I for?
my hope is in thee.
PSALM 39:7 KJV

DAY 153

Demonstrating Love

God, I have the most demanding boss ever. I need to demonstrate the love of Christ, but it can be challenging when my superior is, at times, so hard to please. Give me courage, Lord, to rise above my emotions. Help me to pray for my boss as the Bible tells me to and to serve as though it is an assignment from You. For You, Lord, are my true superior. Bless my boss today, God, and show Your love to him through me. Amen.

Whatever you do, work at it with all your heart,
as working for the Lord, not for human masters.
COLOSSIANS 3:23 NIV

DAY 154
Confidante

Dear God, the Bible tells older women to mentor younger women. That's an element missing from my life. Although my mom did a great job of passing along the life lessons she'd learned, and we have a good relationship, I still need the insight and affirmation of an older woman. Lord, I need a trusted confidante, one who will help me succeed. I ask You to send someone like that my way in fulfillment of Your Word. And let me fill that role myself someday when I have the required résumé. Amen.

May [the aged women] teach the young women to be sober, to love their husbands, to love their children.
TITUS 2:4 KJV

DAY 155

Your Spirit Is on Me

I'm overwhelmed when I think about this verse, Lord. What an amazing declaration. You have poured out Your Spirit on me and filled me from the inside out. You have anointed me to reach my little corner of the world. You have called me to do great things for Your kingdom. What specific plans You've crafted for my life, Father. Your calling is irrevocable. You send me out to those in bondage to proclaim good news, and (even though I'm frightened at times) I choose to go. Use me, Father. With Your Spirit on me, I can do anything. Hallelujah! Amen.

The Spirit of the Lord God is on me, because the Lord has chosen me to bring good news to poor people. He has sent me to heal those with a sad heart. He has sent me to tell those who are being held and those in prison that they can go free.

ISAIAH 61:1 NLV

DAY 156
Letting Go of Bitterness

Bitterness is like cancer, God. It grows and takes over, squeezing out life. I don't want to be marked or consumed by bitterness. Let me not hold to the injustices I've experienced. Help me accept Your healing touch and let go of the beginnings of bitterness in my soul. As Joseph noted in the Old Testament, You can turn things meant for evil into good. Please do that in my life. In Christ's name, amen.

Let all bitterness, wrath, anger, clamor, and evil speaking be put away from you, with all malice.
EPHESIANS 4:31 NKJV

DAY 157
Modest Example

So many people think that modesty is only a clothing issue, but You've shown me that it's so much more. It's an attitude akin to humility, and it's what You want from me. Even in this You set the example for me, Jesus. Help me to follow the pattern You've given me. Amen.

In like manner also, that women adorn themselves in modest apparel, with shamefacedness and sobriety; not with broided hair, or gold, or pearls, or costly array; but (which becometh women professing godliness) with good works.

1 Timothy 2:9–10 kjv

DAY 158
Love in Deed and Truth

Father, it is easy to say the words "I love you," but it is harder to live them. You want Your children to love their enemies. You tell us to love through action and with truth. These are high callings that require Your Holy Spirit working in us. Use me as a vessel of love today in my little corner of the world. Let me love through my deeds and not just with words. Amen.

My little children, let us not love in word,
neither in tongue; but in deed and in truth.
1 John 3:18 KJV

DAY 159
Steward of Grace

Thank You for the gifts You have given me, Lord. I look around at the other believers in my life. We are all gifted in different ways. Help me to be a good steward of the gifts You have entrusted me with in this life. Instead of looking out for myself, may I have opportunities to use my abilities to minister to others. I understand that it is in doing so that I honor You. Amen.

As every man hath received the gift, even so minister the same one to another, as good stewards of the manifold grace of God.

1 PETER 4:10 KJV

DAY 160
A Lasting Promise

So few things last, Lord. I buy a loaf of bread and it's hard within a week. A jug of milk? It's good for seven to ten days at best. Even my vehicles have let me down sooner than I'd hoped. Things in this life just aren't designed to last forever. That's one reason I take such comfort in the idea that Your words aren't just for the here and now (like that loaf of bread) but for ten years from now and even into eternity. It's hard to imagine "forever," Father. I'm trying to wrap my mind around it. But I'm so glad to know that You're a "forever" kind of friend, one I can trust from here on out. Thank You for this declaration that Your words will never pass away. Praise You for that. Amen.

"Heaven and earth will pass away,
but my words will not pass away."
MATTHEW 24:35 ESV

DAY 161
You Say I Can Succeed

The world is full of cheerleaders. I hear them all the time, Lord. They tell me I can get rich quick, that I can lose twenty pounds in a month, that I can lower my interest rate on my credit card and save lots of money. These "cheers" are hyped up and don't ring true. But You, Lord? I love it when You cheer me on! You tell me I can succeed, that I can prosper. You don't offer any get-rich-quick schemes (thank goodness). Instead, You tell me that my success lies in my relationship with You. I'll stick with Your words, Father, that I might experience Your version of success. Amen.

"Keep this Book of the Law always on your lips; meditate on it day and night, so that you may be careful to do everything written in it. Then you will be prosperous and successful."

Joshua 1:8 niv

You're Not a Human Being

Your Word is truthful in all situations, Lord. I can trust that what You say will be fulfilled. You're not like the people I've known who say one thing but mean another. Sometimes humans (myself included) have great intentions when they make promises, but they don't follow through. Some say, "Sure, I'll be there for you," and then they're not. But You're not like that, Father. Every promise You've ever spoken (either in Your Word or whispered in my ear) is solid-gold truth. I'm so grateful. Amen.

"God is not human, that he should lie, not a human being, that he should change his mind. Does he speak and then not act? Does he promise and not fulfill?"

NUMBERS 23:19 NIV

DAY 163
You Speak to Me

They are the age-old questions, Lord: How can I hear Your voice? Is it really still and small, or are Your words booming, earthshaking? Can I hear You in the cries of a newborn or in the stillness of a stream trickling over rocks? Will I find Your thoughts in the Bible and carved on my heart? Truth is, I can hear only if my spiritual ears are opened, so today I offer them to You. Speak, Lord, in any way You choose. Bolster my courage. Lift my heart. Whisper, "Attagirl," like only You can. I'm listening, Father. Ears wide open. Amen.

"Have I not commanded you? Be strong and courageous.
Do not be afraid; do not be discouraged, for the LORD
your God will be with you wherever you go."

JOSHUA 1:9 NIV

DAY 164
An Heir to the King

Heavenly Father, thank You for adopting me as an heir to the King of kings! You provided a way for me to come before You, holy God. Christ carried my sin as His burden. It was nailed to the cross and has been forgiven forever, once and for all. Thank You for the abundant life that is mine because I am Yours. I praise You for viewing me through a lens called grace. Amen.

That being justified by his grace, we should be made heirs according to the hope of eternal life.
TITUS 3:7 KJV

DAY 165
Amazing Grace

Lord, I get so caught up in trying to do good works sometimes. I need to remember that I am saved by grace. You are pleased with me simply because I believe in Your Son, Jesus, and I have accepted Him as my Savior. You do not bless me or withhold good gifts based on my performance. Remind me of Your amazing grace, and make me gracious with others. In Jesus' name I pray, amen.

For by grace are ye saved through faith;
and that not of yourselves: it is the gift of God:
not of works, lest any man should boast.

EPHESIANS 2:8–9 KJV

DAY 166
Special to the Father

How can I doubt my worth in Your eyes, Father? You know the number of hairs on my head. You created me, and You said that Your creation is very good. When I'm tempted to get down on myself, remind me that I am special to You, and there's no one just like me. Amen.

In the multitude of my thoughts within
me thy comforts delight my soul.
PSALM 94:19 KJV

DAY 167
All of Me

When You were asked what the greatest commandment was, You did not evade the question. You answered clearly, Jesus. I am to love the Lord my God with all of my heart, soul, mind, and strength. I am to love my God with all of me. There should be nothing left over when I am finished loving God. No crumbs I feed to the idols that crave my attention. It is all for You. Amen.

And thou shalt love the Lord thy God with all thy heart,
and with all thy soul, and with all thy mind, and with
all thy strength: this is the first commandment.
MARK 12:30 KJV

DAY 168
A Thankful Heart

Lord, everything good in my life comes from You. Often I forget to thank You. I am thankful for Your provision and Your protection. I am thankful for my family and friends. I am most of all thankful for the joy of my salvation, which comes through Christ. Give me a grateful heart, I pray. Let me always remember that every good and perfect gift comes from Your hand. Amen.

And let the peace of God rule in your hearts, to the which also ye are called in one body; and be ye thankful.
COLOSSIANS 3:15 KJV

DAY 169
In Harm's Way

Dear God, so many missionaries are in harm's way. They face terrorist threats, unsanitary living conditions, and even dangerous animals or illnesses that I can't begin to fathom. Please protect them, Father. They've willingly taken these risks so that others might know Your love. Keep them under Your wing of safety. Amen.

Unto the upright there ariseth light in the darkness: he is gracious, and full of compassion, and righteous.

PSALM 112:4 KJV

I'm so grateful that You're speaking words of life to my heart, Father. There's so much negativity in this world. Sometimes I think the enemy of my soul works overtime to bring me down. But I won't let him. I'll tune out his voice and listen only to what You're saying. What's that? Oh, You want me to know that I have purpose, that my life is going to be rich and full? I'm grateful for the reminder, Lord! Praise You for speaking words of abundant life. Amen.

May you experience the love of Christ, though it is too great to understand fully. Then you will be made complete with all the fullness of life and power that comes from God.
EPHESIANS 3:19 NLT

The Hairs of My Head

My ability to remember details appears to be waning, Father. Sometimes it's all I can do to remember a friend's birthday or a bill that needs to be paid. The little things slip right by me at times. But You, Lord? You never forget. You're in the details, 100 percent. It boggles my mind to think that You've numbered the hairs of my head. (I lost a few just this morning, Father—but You already knew that!) Even in an ever-changing environment, You still keep track. Oh, to be more like You, Lord. Give me eyes to see (and take care of) the details in my life. Thank You in advance. Amen.

"And even the very hairs of your
head are all numbered."
—Matthew 10:30 niv

DAY 172
That You May Proclaim

I'll proclaim it, Lord! I'll shout it out from the rooftop, in fact. You are a most excellent Father, worthy of praise. Grow my boldness, Father, that I might willingly share with all who need to know that there is a God who can pull them out of dark places and into marvelous light. If I don't work up the courage to share, who will? You've called me and set me apart for this very purpose, that I might make this proclamation. So today I will tell others how amazing You are. Thank You for making me a hope giver, Father. I want to be like You. Amen.

But you are a chosen race, a royal priesthood,
a holy nation, a people for his own possession,
that you may proclaim the excellencies of him who
called you out of darkness into his marvelous light.

1 Peter 2:9 esv

DAY 173
Forgetting What Lies Behind

I tend to crane my neck, Lord, keeping an eye on what's just happened as I plow forward. Help me to keep my focus on You, Father. Knowing You're in charge, knowing You have plans for me, helps me forget the things I've experienced and focus solely on You. Now that's a great perspective, Lord! Amen.

I do not mean that I am already as God wants me to be. I have not yet reached that goal, but I continue trying to reach it and to make it mine. Christ wants me to do that, which is the reason he made me his. Brothers and sisters, I know that I have not yet reached that goal, but there is one thing I always do. Forgetting the past and straining toward what is ahead, I keep trying to reach the goal and get the prize for which God called me through Christ to the life above.

PHILIPPIANS 3:12–14 NCV

DAY 174
Blessing Those Who Hurt You

God, when someone hurts me, I don't feel like blessing him or her. Remind me what Your Word teaches about love. Love keeps no record of wrongs. Love forgives. It restores. Love tries again. Love lets it go. Love blesses even when it's not my turn to bless! Give me a spirit of love that trumps evil. And allow me to bless those who hurt me. I can only do so in Your power. Amen.

Not rendering evil for evil, or railing for railing:
but contrariwise blessing; knowing that ye are
thereunto called, that ye should inherit a blessing.
1 PETER 3:9 KJV

DAY 175
Tithing

Father, You tell me to test You with my tithe. If I give it generously, You will bless my household. I will find it overflowing with blessing. There will not be enough room to contain all of it. I imagine the windows of heaven opening and blessings just pouring, pouring, pouring down on me! You are not a God who sprinkles blessings or gives them in little pinches or samples. You are an extravagant giver. Amen.

Bring ye all the tithes into the storehouse. . .and prove me now herewith, saith the LORD of hosts, if I will not open you the windows of heaven, and pour you out a blessing.

MALACHI 3:10 KJV

A Woman Who Fears the Lord

God, I want to be a Proverbs 31 woman. My focus should not be on external beauty or the clothing and jewelry that I wear. Rather, may others notice my heart that is forever seeking You. I want nothing more than to be known as a woman of God. Protect me from vanity. Outward beauty is not lasting, but a beautiful spirit is. I meditate upon Your Word now, Lord. I want to honor You. Amen.

Favour is deceitful, and beauty is vain: but a woman that feareth the Lord, she shall be praised.
PROVERBS 31:30 KJV

DAY 177
Right Paths

The right path is often the one less traveled. I am learning this, Father, oh so slowly. You will always lead me in the right path. You will never lead me astray. I have been at the crossroads many times, and I will face such choices again and again. Keep my heart focused on You so that I might be led down pleasant paths, paths that will glorify my King. Amen.

I have taught thee in the way of wisdom;
I have led thee in right paths.
PROVERBS 4:11 KJV

DAY 178
When to Remain Silent

Heavenly Father, Your Word says that the tongue has great power. My words can help or harm. There are times when silence is best. Help me to know the difference between times I should speak and times I should keep still. I pray for wisdom as I go through this day. I want my speech to honor You. Put a guard over my lips, I pray. Amen.

In the multitude of words there wanteth not sin:
but he that refraineth his lips is wise.
PROVERBS 10:19 KJV

DAY 179
Known by God

Not only did You keep careful watch over me in the womb, Lord, but (like You did for Jeremiah) You consecrated me—set me apart—to do special things for You. What an amazing revelation, to know that I was called, chosen, and set apart even when my very bones were forming! How special are Your plans for my life, Father, that You took the time to set them in motion even before I drew my first breath. You are truly remarkable, Lord! Amen.

"Before I formed you in the womb I knew you,
and before you were born I consecrated you;
I appointed you a prophet to the nations."

JEREMIAH 1:5 ESV

DAY 180
Each One, Chosen

You picked me, Lord! Of all the people in the world (and there are billions), You handpicked me to be a member of the family. It feels so good to be wanted. Needed. Loved. Thank You for arranging Your family across this great big globe as one unit. I have brothers and sisters as far as the eye can see. I need them—and they need me. Together, we are an unstoppable force in You, Lord. Praise You for that. Amen.

But in fact God has placed the parts in the body, every one of them, just as he wanted them to be.

1 CORINTHIANS 12:18 NIV

DAY 181

Spoken into Existence

Father, I get it! You spoke the world (and everything in it) into existence. Your words brought even the tiniest ladybug to life. Before I was born, You spoke me into existence and knew the paths my life would take. Now, Father, You're teaching me to speak things into existence, to follow the pattern You've set for me. I can look at the situations in my life and speak words of life over them. When I do, the same creative power flows forth. Thank You, Lord, for the ability to speak life. Amen.

In the beginning God created the heavens and the earth.

GENESIS 1:1 NIV

DAY 182

Applying Instruction

God, give me ears to hear. Sharpen my senses and make me wise. I am often proud. I think I know it all. But I don't. I need instruction from You. I know this comes in many forms. . .through reading and meditating on Your Word, through Your people, and through circumstances. Help me to be a good listener and to apply the instruction You send my way. I want to be wise, Father. Amen.

Hear counsel, and receive instruction,
that thou mayest be wise in thy latter end.
PROVERBS 19:20 KJV

DAY 183
Generosity

Father, the psalmist declares that he has never seen the righteous forsaken or his children going hungry. This inspires me. I know that You bless those who give. I want to leave a legacy of generosity for my children or for others who are influenced by my life. What they see me practicing regarding giving will impact their choices. May we be a generous family, always looking for opportunities to show mercy. Amen.

I have been young, and now am old; yet have I not seen the righteous forsaken, nor his seed begging bread. He is ever merciful, and lendeth; and his seed is blessed.

PSALM 37:25–26 KJV

DAY 184
Christlikeness

There's such a fine line between self-esteem and arrogance. Sometimes I have trouble distinguishing between the two. Father, You created me in Your image. For that I am thankful, but I need to remember that I'm not perfect. Help me not to be proud but to daily strive to be more like You. Amen.

When pride cometh, then cometh shame:
but with the lowly is wisdom.
PROVERBS 11:2 KJV

DAY 185
A Testimony

My life is a song of praise to You, my faithful Father, the giver of life! When people hear my testimony of Your goodness, may they come to know You. I want others to notice the difference in me and wonder why I have such joy, such peace. May I point them to You, Lord, and may they trust in You for salvation. You are the way, the truth, and the life. Amen.

And he hath put a new song in my mouth,
even praise unto our God: many shall see it,
and fear, and shall trust in the Lord.

PSALM 40:3 KJV

DAY 186
Finding Time to Rest

I find it difficult to even sit down to a meal, Father. Resting seems like such a far-fetched notion. I know You want me to find time to rest and spend time with You, but I'm on the go constantly, and I still don't get everything done. Please help me, Lord, to make resting a priority. Amen.

Cast thy burden upon the LORD, and he shall sustain thee: he shall never suffer the righteous to be moved.
PSALM 55:22 KJV

DAY 187
Showing That I Love God

How do I show that I love You, God? It must be more than merely a phrase I use in prayer. The way I show it is to keep Your commandments. I need Your strength for this. I fail every day. Renew my desire to live according to Your principles. They are not suggestions. They are commands. Honoring them will cause me to see You at work in my life. I love You, Lord. Amen.

He that hath my commandments, and keepeth them, he it is that loveth me: and he that loveth me shall be loved of my Father, and I will love him, and will manifest myself to him.

JOHN 14:21 KJV

DAY 188
Harmful Relationships

Lord, I generally think of relationships as being between people, and I fail to remember that my relationships to things can seriously affect how I react to people. For instance, sometimes I get so involved in a television show that I fail to give needed attention to my family. Forgive me, Father. Be in charge of my relationships. Amen.

And beside this, giving all diligence, add to your faith virtue; and to virtue knowledge; and to knowledge temperance; and to temperance patience; and to patience godliness; and to godliness brotherly kindness; and to brotherly kindness charity.

2 PETER 1:5–7 KJV

DAY 189
Prospering in the Details

I don't always remember that all things work together for good. Sometimes I get lost in the details, in the nitty-gritty. Oh, but You've reminded me that I can prosper, even in the minutia. When the day is overwhelmingly busy. When the car breaks down. When the kids won't stop fighting. When the boss is pushing me to recheck my work. Even then, Lord, You're there. Your plan to bring prosperity to my life often takes me to places where I'm inundated with details. But there You are, Father, in the midst of them all. How grateful I am! Amen.

*And we know that in all things God works for
the good of those who love him, who have
been called according to his purpose.*

ROMANS 8:28 NIV

DAY 190
Supernatural Strength

It's fascinating to think about, Lord. Your plans for my life are fully in place, even when I'm exhausted, even when I don't feel like I can put one foot in front of the other. After all, I reach the end of myself pretty quickly, as You well know. I hit a wall. During those times, I can't think clearly, can't move forward. Then You come along. You miraculously give me energy. It comes on me in a supernatural way and even surprises me. With Your strength, I'm able to do more than ever before. Or, I should say that You're able to do more through me. Today, I give You my weariness. I ask You to breathe on me, Holy Spirit, and energize me. Make me a vibrant channel You can flow through. I submit myself to that process. Amen.

He gives strength to the weary and
increases the power of the weak.

Isaiah 40:29 niv

DAY 191
I'm Sure of What I Hope For

Confident. Sure. These words propel me, Father. I want to remain confident, even during the rough seasons. I want to square my shoulders, look my problems in the eye, and be absolutely convinced You're going to come through for me. This takes faith, I know, but You are the author of faith. So that's what I ask for today, Lord. Give me faith to believe for assurance. Give me faith to stand strong when others around me are falling. May I be sure of what I hope for, Father. Amen.

"But blessed is the one who trusts in the Lord, whose confidence is in him."

JEREMIAH 17:7 NIV

DAY 192
Your Eye Is on Me

What is it like, Lord, to sit in heaven and watch over Your children on earth? I would imagine it's like watching toddlers at play sometimes. What a patient Father You are! It's remarkable to think that You can see all of us at once: billions of people on Planet Earth, and Your eyes see all. You've also crafted specific plans for each of us, and You're always close by to make sure those plans come to fruition—even when we get off course. If we wander from the path, You're right there to lead us back again. What a loving Father You are. Thanks for watching over us. Amen.

I will instruct you and teach you in the way you should go:
I will counsel you with my eye upon you.

PSALM 32:8 ESV

DAY 193
His Purposes

God, it's remarkable to think about the fact that You are capable of doing all things. There's not a thing You've ever tried that You didn't accomplish. Me? I try and fail all the time. I can't even imagine what it must feel like to have a 100 percent success rate. (How amazing would that be?) Because You're the ultimate example of success, I know I can trust You to successfully plan my future. You won't make any mistakes. Me? If You'd put me in charge, I'm pretty sure I would've messed things up in a big way. Today I'm so grateful that no purpose of Yours can be thwarted. Amen.

"I know that you can do all things, and that no purpose of yours can be thwarted."

JOB 42:2 ESV

DAY 194
Not in Himself

The world tells me to look within, Lord. I'm told that everything I need to know about myself, for myself, is already inside me. Oh Father, what a foolish notion! The answers aren't found in me. I can plan and devise all I like, but the only true answers are found in You. If I set my own course, I'm sure to land in a ditch. You direct my path. You make the plans. I'll do my best to lean close and listen as You lead me along a better path. Amen.

Lord, I know that people's lives are not their own;
it is not for them to direct their steps.
JEREMIAH 10:23 NIV

DAY 195
Stop and Know

Be still. A call to quiet my restless mind—to pause in my endless pursuits. *Know that You are God.* You are almighty. You are Lord. Regardless of what goes on in the world today, Father, I can be still and relish the knowledge that the God who created and controls the universe also resides in my heart. And Your plans will not be shaken—even when my fears shake me to the very core. Deepen my trust, Father; take my head knowledge to my heart so I can feel Your presence in my life, to be still and know that You are God. Amen.

"Be still, and know that I am God. I will be exalted among the nations, I will be exalted in the earth!"

PSALM 46:10 ESV

DAY 196
Abiding

Heavenly Father, as Your Son, Jesus was the model of perfect obedience to You. Although I cannot expect to be perfect, I can follow in Jesus' path of obedience. I can make Your commandments the framework of my life. By living under Your commands in obedience, I place myself in the shelter of Your love, abiding there, remaining there. I can't do it alone, Father. I pray for an obedient heart. I pray for the power of the Holy Spirit to resist the temptation to follow my own path. I bow to Your wisdom in knowing what is best for me. Amen.

"By this my Father is glorified, that you bear much fruit and so prove to be my disciples. As the Father has loved me, so have I loved you. Abide in my love."

JOHN 15:8–9 ESV

DAY 197
Too Deep for Words

Father, this earthly life can be overwhelming. Suffering abounds. It's hard to maintain hope of a bright future when the present seems so dismal. At times it's even difficult to put the weight of what I feel into words. But Your Holy Spirit intercedes for us. From heaven You listen, and You're faithful. Your plans will come to pass. You keep Your promises. You are good, and You desire ultimate good for Your children. Remind me of Your love, Father. When my words fail, let the groanings of the Spirit be my voice. You'll hear them loud and clear! Amen.

Likewise the Spirit helps us in our weakness. For we do not know what to pray for as we ought, but the Spirit himself intercedes for us with groanings too deep for words.

ROMANS 8:26 ESV

DAY 198
Lie Down and Sleep

Father, when I can't fall asleep, night becomes endless. My mind fills the silence with unspoken thoughts about troubles. It fills the darkness with images of an uncertain future. But it doesn't have to be like this. King David knew more chaos and danger, yet he trusted in Your care and found sleep. Nothing can happen to me that You have not foreseen; I can close my eyes and rest in Your will. When I can't fall asleep, let Your promises of love fall over me like the words of a lullaby. Let Your peace surround me like a warm blanket. You are God. You are good. I trust in Your care and find sleep. Amen.

In peace I will both lie down and sleep;
for you alone, O LORD, make me dwell in safety.
PSALM 4:8 ESV

DAY 199
Ask for It

Wisdom, Father, can be elusive. What is Your will for my life? How do I handle the trials this world throws at me with joy and grace? My lack of wisdom draws me ever closer to You. You have all the answers because You have written my life's story. Today I want to ask for wisdom, Father. But before I do, I need a boost in faith. In my head I say I trust You; please root out any doubt residing in my heart. Let greater wisdom begin with realizing my need for You in all things. Amen.

If any of you lacks wisdom, let him ask God, who gives generously to all without reproach, and it will be given him. But let him ask in faith, with no doubting, for the one who doubts is like a wave of the sea that is driven and tossed by the wind.

JAMES 1:5–6 ESV

DAY 200
Without Sight

Lord Jesus, we can all be Thomas at times. We ask for signs. We want proof. If only we could touch Your nail-pierced hands... The truth is, believing without seeing is hard. You knew this. You knew that many believers would come to faith without seeing You, the proof of Your resurrection, until heaven. So You spoke words of encouragement. By believing without seeing, I am blessed. And You have not left me without the help of Your Spirit. You "show" Yourself to me in countless ways. Through Your provision. Through Your faithful presence in my life. Through the beauty of Your creation. Through answered prayers. Lord, You are undeniable. Amen.

Jesus said to him, "Have you believed because you have seen me? Blessed are those who have not seen and yet have believed."

JOHN 20:29 ESV

DAY 201
Perfect in Knowledge

Lord, I remember so clearly the times I had to take tests in school, how I prayed for Your divine intervention. I wanted everything I'd learned to root itself in my heart so that I could have a ready answer for every question. How marvelous to realize that You are perfect in knowledge. There's not a test question out there that You can't answer. My mind can't fathom Your ability, Father, but I marvel in the fact that Your ways are perfect. With that in mind, I choose to trust You as I move forward with Your hand in mine. Amen.

"Do you know how the clouds hang poised,
those wonders of him who has perfect knowledge?"
JOB 37:16 NIV

DAY 202
Called Forth

There's a calling on my life, Lord. I sense it. I feel it. I appreciate it. I choose to respond to it. You've called me with a unique and personalized calling, one that fits like a satin glove. I hear what You're whispering in my ear, that Your intense love for me propelled You to stir my heart to action. Thank You, Father. Knowing that the King of the universe has taken the time to plot, strategize, and implement a plan for my life is amazing. What a blessing! Amen.

"Who has done this and carried it through, calling forth
the generations from the beginning? I, the LORD—
with the first of them and with the last—I am he."
ISAIAH 41:4 NIV

DAY 203
You Stretched Out the Heavens

I can almost picture it now, Lord. Your mighty hand, grabbing hold over the corners of heaven and tugging them into place. You stretched, and things were established. The same has been true in my life, Lord. Your plans have stretched me beyond what I thought I was capable of. Your wisdom has grown me into someone who trusts You more, walks on water with greater assurance, and looks toward the future as a hopeful place. How can I ever thank You enough for growing me into a stronger woman of God? My heart is Yours, Lord. Amen.

"He made the earth by his power; he founded the world by his wisdom and stretched out the heavens by his understanding."

JEREMIAH 51:15 NIV

DAY 204
You Are the Potter

You are my Potter, Father. You've placed me on the wheel, a formless lump of clay. With Your hands firmly guiding the process, You've shaped me into a visionary, one who sees the vast possibilities for my life. I love what I'm seeing. As You morph me from season to season, I'm growing—spiritually, emotionally, and psychologically. I give You full permission to continue Your work, that Your plan for my life might be all You intended. Thank You, my Potter! Amen.

Woe to those who go to great depths to hide their plans from the LORD, who do their work in darkness and think, "Who sees us? Who will know?" You turn things upside down, as if the potter were thought to be like the clay! Shall what is formed say to the one who formed it, "You did not make me"? Can the pot say to the potter, "You know nothing"?

ISAIAH 29:15–16 NIV

DAY 205
Broken in the Depths

What an amazing scripture, Lord! By Your knowledge, the oceans, lakes, rivers, streams, and ponds were broken up. Each became its own entity. I know from personal experience that the breaking process isn't always easy, but the outcome is always worth it. Today I give You permission, as You lay forth the plans for my life, to break me in the depths. Break my heart for what breaks Yours. Break my will, so that my selfish desires will fade. Break my pride, that I may be more like You. May I, in the brokenness, become more like You, my Creator. Amen.

By wisdom the LORD laid the earth's foundations,
by understanding he set the heavens in place;
by his knowledge the watery depths were divided,
and the clouds let drop the dew.
PROVERBS 3:19–20 NIV

DAY 206
Carving Channels

Father, what a revelation to know that You go ahead of me and actually carve out channels through the rocks. I would be like a miner lost in the darkened hollows of the shaft if not for You! How remarkable, to think that Your eye sees even the most beautiful gems in the rock You're carving out. Are there diamonds along my path, Father? If so, give me Your vision to see as the road ahead is carved. What a beautiful story You're writing, Lord! I'm so honored You would go to such trouble for me. Amen.

*"He cuts out channels in the rocks,
and his eye sees every precious thing."*

JOB 28:10 NKJV

Wisdom and Might

I am created in Your image, Father, and I'm so grateful. I know that wisdom and power are Yours, but I also know that as Your child, I can be wise and powerful too. (One of the perks of being Your child!) Your counsel is the best. I know, because I've applied it to my life on so many occasions. But I'm glad You're teaching me to counsel others as well. May Your understanding and Your wisdom be mine as I walk this road You've laid before me. Have I mentioned how grateful I am that I'm Your daughter, Lord? Amen.

"To God belong wisdom and power;
counsel and understanding are his."

JOB 12:13 NIV

DAY 208
A Strong Support

It's fascinating to think about Your eyesight, Lord. How is it possible to see all of the universe—every planet, every continent, every country, every city, every neighborhood, every home—all at once? I marvel at the very idea. It brings a smile to my face when I think about the fact that You are watching those of us who've committed our lives to You, so that You can bring strength. Please look on me today, Father. Give me the strength I need to travel down this road You've placed me on. Thanks for keeping such a good eye on me, Lord. Amen.

"For the eyes of the LORD range throughout
the earth to strengthen those whose
hearts are fully committed to him."
2 CHRONICLES 16:9 NIV

You've placed so many wonderful people in my life, Lord. I've come to know so many. I've discovered, though, that to be known requires a more intimate relationship. That's what You're asking of me as Your plans are laid out before me: to know and be known. May I know You more as I delve into a deeper relationship with You. As Your plans for my life unfold (and what fun, to discover these plans day by day), I feel like I'm getting to know You even more. I'm also getting to know myself, which has been great fun—though a little frightening at times, since I'm so far from perfect. Oh, to know and be known by my Creator! Oh, to walk in intimate relationship with others. What a privilege. Thank You, Father. Amen.

*"I am the good shepherd; I know
my sheep and my sheep know me."*

JOHN 10:14 NIV

DAY 210
Living and Active

When I open my Bible, Lord, it's almost like the words jump out at me. I can see them as a mighty sword, piercing my heart and cutting to the very place where I need them most. It's an amazing thing, Father, to see how You match the verses with the situations I'm walking through. On those days when I'm feeling a little lost, when I'm not sure where the road is taking me, out springs a verse, giving clear direction. Your Word is alive, Lord! It's breathing. It's active. It's relatable, even in the twenty-first century. How can I ever thank You enough for speaking life to Your children? Praise You for Your Word. Amen.

For the word of God is alive and active. Sharper than any double-edged sword, it penetrates even to dividing soul and spirit, joints and marrow; it judges the thoughts and attitudes of the heart.

HEBREWS 4:12 NIV

DAY 211
You See My Steps

Remember that time, Lord, when I missed a step and fell? As I careened downward, I felt the pain of impact. Oh, how it hurt; how I wished I'd seen that stair step in advance to better navigate my way. You healed my broken body, but You also taught me a life lesson. All of my steps are visible to You. Even in the darkest night as I feel my way along, You see clearly. Move me with confidence toward the future You have planned for me, Father. Even when I can't see where I'm headed, I know that You do. Every step I take is visible, even the bumbling ones. I give You my feet. Be my compass. Be my guide. I will follow where You lead. Amen.

"His eyes are on the ways of mortals;
he sees their every step."

JOB 34:21 NIV

DAY 212
Understanding Your Will

So often I rail against what I do not understand. It's hard to move forward when what's in front of me makes no sense at all. But You're teaching me, Father, that one thing is a given: You have my best interest at heart. So, I choose to keep moving, even when I'm perplexed by the twists and turns in the road. I don't want to be thoughtless. I want every step in my journey to be carefully thought out so that I know without a doubt what You're wanting me to do. If I begin to veer in the wrong direction, please take hold of my hand and lead me back to the right road. May I listen carefully, so that I can understand, Lord. Thank You for Your guidance! Amen.

Show me the right path, O Lord;
point out the road for me to follow.
PSALM 25:4 NLT

DAY 213
Victory!

I love a good victory, Father, whether it's at a ball game, during a volatile political season, or in an argument with an adversary. But there's a greater victory than the ones I see in the temporal realm. When You died on the cross, Jesus, the ultimate victory over sin and death was won. This victory leads to eternal life for all who call on Your name. How can I ever thank You enough for winning that battle on my behalf, Lord? I commit myself to enthusiastically share the good news of what You've done so that others can share in this victory too. Amen.

But thank God! He gives us victory over sin and death through our Lord Jesus Christ. So, my dear brothers and sisters, be strong and immovable. Always work enthusiastically for the Lord, for you know that nothing you do for the Lord is ever useless.

1 CORINTHIANS 15:57–58 NLT

DAY 214
Right Paths

Choices, choices. They're everywhere! I could turn to the right. Or the left. I could go forward. Or backward. I could take this job. Or that job. Or even that other job. I could date this person. Or that person. Or the other person. With so many paths in front of me (and so many voices urging me to go this way or that), I could find myself headed in the wrong direction in a hurry. Today I commit myself to listen carefully to Your voice alone, so that I can take the right road. And as I step out onto it, I will receive strength for the journey that only You can give. With every step, I will do my best to bring honor and glory to Your name. Amen.

He renews my strength. He guides me along
right paths, bringing honor to his name.
PSALM 23:3 NLT

DAY 215
A Face-to-Face Meeting

So many of the situations in my life are muddy, Lord. Unclear. Blurry. Sometimes I wish I had a magic mirror like the ones in fairy tales, so that I could clearly see what's coming. Thank goodness that You know. And though my vision is imperfect, there's coming a day when everything will make perfect sense. I will see You face-to-face and receive all of the answers to the lingering questions in my life. Until that day, I choose to trust in Your plans, Father, even when they look a bit fuzzy around the edges. Amen.

When I awake, I will see
you face to face and be satisfied.
PSALM 17:15 NLT

DAY 216
Until It Is Finally Finished

You're a "never give up" kind of God, and I love that about You. When You start things, You finish them. I wish I could say I had that attribute, but many times I begin projects and give up halfway through. I throw in the towel often before I've even given things a chance. You won't give up on me, Lord, even when I feel like giving up on myself. Whew. That's a comfort. Your work will continue all the way to completion. I don't know what the "completed" me will look like, but You do—and You've already begun the work to get me there. Thanks for hanging in there! Amen.

I am certain that God, who began the good work within you, will continue his work until it is finally finished on the day when Christ Jesus returns.
PHILIPPIANS 1:6 NLT

DAY 217
To the End of the Age

It's probably a good thing that I don't know how long I'll live, Lord. I don't know the number of my days, but You do. I'm not counting down the minutes, but I am doing my best to live each day with purpose, ready to see Your plans fulfilled in my life. Best of all, I'm enjoying getting to know You more with each passing day. No matter how many years I have left, every one will be spent with Your hand in mine. How remarkable to know that the Creator of the universe cares enough about me to walk with me, every day of my life. Praise You for that, Lord. Amen.

"And surely I am with you always,
to the very end of the age."

MATTHEW 28:20 NIV

DAY 218
I Live by Faith

It's not about me anymore, Lord. It's all about You. Oh, I know—it used to be about me. Always. My way or the highway. But those days are gone. The old me has vanished. In her place: Jesus Christ, Your Son! This new outlook has taken some getting used to. (I was, after all, looking out for me, myself, and I for a very long time.) But, after all You've done for me, how could I desire any other path? I choose to live by faith in the one who gave Himself for me. May every attitude be a reflection of that decision, Father. Amen.

I have been crucified with Christ and I no longer live, but Christ lives in me. The life I now live in the body, I live by faith in the Son of God, who loved me and gave himself for me.
GALATIANS 2:20 NIV

DAY 219
Your Great Love

It's the ultimate verse, Lord, the one we hang all of our hopes and dreams on. Your love—that vast, immeasurable, transforming love—offers us new hope. Your plan for us always included a happily-ever-after with You. What an amazing romancer You are! You woo us to You then provide life eternal. But what a sacrifice You made, sending Your Son so that all of this would be possible. There are no words to express my gratitude, but I will try, Lord. With all of my life, my actions, my thoughts, my motivations, I will try. Amen.

For God so loved the world that he gave his one and only Son, that whoever believes in him shall not perish but have eternal life.
JOHN 3:16 NIV

DAY 220
Wherever We Go

I'm remembering my childhood, Lord—how I would climb into the backseat of the car and let my parents take me from place to place. I didn't always know where we were headed, but from the moment I got in that car, I knew I would be safe. The same is true with You, Father. Wherever I go, whether it's to a local supermarket or a mission field halfway across the globe, You're behind the wheel, carrying me safely to where I need to be. What a comfort, to trust in the One who created me to lead me safely on. Amen.

"Be strong and courageous. Do not be afraid or terrified because of them, for the LORD your God goes with you; he will never leave you nor forsake you."

DEUTERONOMY 31:6 NIV

DAY 221
Your Good Pleasure

The kingdom. Oh, how I love speaking that word. *Kingdom.* Sometimes I feel like a princess in a castle tower, surveying all of the lands below that belong to her father, the king. You are the great and mighty King, Lord, and I'm in awe of Your kingdom—both the earthly kingdom and the heavenly kingdom to come. What truly awes me is that You've chosen to give all of this: the pleasures of a relationship with You here on earth and a heavenly home besides. You must really care a lot about me, Lord. I am Your humble daughter, completely wowed by her Daddy God. Amen.

"Do not be afraid, little flock, for your Father has been pleased to give you the kingdom."

LUKE 12:32 NIV

DAY 222
Broken Chains

Wow, what a picture of Your power, Lord! You've broken through gates of bronze and bars of iron to get to me. Even when I was in my deepest, darkest place, You came barreling through, ready to release my chains. And all so that I could have a future. You didn't want to see me bound up, Father, living below my potential. That's the kind of unfailing love You had for me then and have for me even now. You've always wanted to lift me to higher places. Praise You for Your great, inspiring passion for Your children. Amen.

Then they cried to the LORD in their trouble, and he saved them from their distress. He brought them out of darkness, the utter darkness, and broke away their chains. Let them give thanks to the LORD for his unfailing love and his wonderful deeds for mankind, for he breaks down gates of bronze and cuts through bars of iron.

PSALM 107:13–16 NIV

DAY 223
Wise One

Sometimes I feel like a little sponge, Lord. I sit there on the counter, dry as a bone, wondering why my life isn't productive. Then I remember why things are going so poorly. I've ceased to spend time with You and in Your Word. So, I race back to Your arms, ready to admit just how much I need You. You brush away every tear and whisper words of great caring into my ears. Only when I spend adequate time with You will I acquire the necessary wisdom to get through the narrow channels in my life, Lord. So today I choose to remain close. May I be like that little sponge, soaking up all the wisdom I can, both today and in all the days to come. Amen.

Get all the advice and instruction you can,
so you will be wise the rest of your life.
PROVERBS 19:20 NLT

DAY 224
Free Indeed

I love the word *truly*, Lord. When You set me free from my past, my addictions, my failures, my woes, my bad attitudes, my habits, my poor relationships, You *truly* set me free. Indeed. How foolish would I be to turn back now, when You've broken chains that held me bound and released me to new life in You? Oh Father, You've brought me so far. I don't even like to look back to the way things used to be, except to learn from my mistakes. You've got such an amazing future planned out for me. I wouldn't want to miss a thing. So I'll stand on the outside of those prison walls, forever grateful You were willing to rescue me, Lord. Truly! Amen.

"So if the Son sets you free, you are truly free."

John 8:36 nlt

DAY 225
You Go Before Me

How secure I felt as a child, Lord, when my mother or father would hold my hand and lead me alongside them. Their long, confident strides gave me courage to trust in where we were headed. The same is true with You. Your strides are long and confident and often stretch far beyond mine, but with Your hand in mine, I feel as secure as I did all those years ago. I'm completely confident that You won't take off running and leave me in the dust. Even when You step out in front of me, You stick close. You care far too much about me to leave me on my own. What a wonderful Father You are! Amen.

"Do not be afraid or discouraged, for the LORD will personally go ahead of you. He will be with you; he will neither fail you nor abandon you."

DEUTERONOMY 31:8 NLT

DAY 226
For Each New Day

Every day there is something for which I can offer You praise, dear God! To begin with, we have the promise of a fresh start—a new opportunity to serve You. Throughout the day You show Your majesty in a multitude of ways. You are an awesome God! Amen.

And of his fulness have all we received, and grace for grace.
JOHN 1:16 KJV

DAY 227
The Weight of Glory

Oh, how the weight of my troubles can drag me down, Father. Sometimes I feel like I'm down on my knees, crawling along. But I'm grateful today for a different kind of weight—the weight of Your glory. You're developing me, Lord, and forming me into Your image. Thank You for fixing my eyes on the things I cannot see so that I can freely walk toward You. Amen.

For our present troubles are small and won't last very long. Yet they produce for us a glory that vastly outweighs them and will last forever! So we don't look at the troubles we can see now; rather, we fix our gaze on things that cannot be seen. For the things we see now will soon be gone, but the things we cannot see will last forever.

2 Corinthians 4:17–18 nlt

DAY 228
Wide Vision

It's such a relief to know that Your vision is wide, Father. You can see from one end of the universe to the other, from every star to every planet to the next breath I'm going to take. You see it all and orchestrate it with Your majestic hand. Because I know Your vision is remarkable, I can count on You to lead and guide. If You can see what's hiding beyond the farthest star, surely You can see what the future holds for me, Your child. Praise You, Lord! Amen.

For he views the ends of the earth and
sees everything under the heavens.
JOB 28:24 NIV

DAY 229
New Compassions Every Day

I get it, Lord. I get why You don't want me to go to bed angry. You don't want to let the woes of one day spill over into the next. When I fall asleep in a peaceful state, I can awake to new beginnings. In the same way, I'm grateful that You don't go to bed angry with me when I've had a less than stellar day. You love me, forgive me, give me a pat on the back, and promise that Your compassions will be new tomorrow morning. What a faithful God You are. Left to my own devices, I would get stuck in the angst of today. But with You, my future is secure, because Your compassions never fail. Thank You, Lord! Amen.

Because of the LORD's great love we are not consumed, for his compassions never fail. They are new every morning; great is your faithfulness.
LAMENTATIONS 3:22–23 NIV

DAY 230
Passport in Heaven

Traveling is so much fun, Lord. I love the journeys I've taken in my life—whether by car, boat, or plane. Getting to my destination is half the fun! The same is true in my journey with You, Father. You're leading me toward the most beautiful destination of all: heaven. Oh, how I'm enjoying the journey, and I feel sure (based on what I've read in Your Word) that the destination will be beyond my wildest dreams. I can almost picture it now. Best of all, my passport is ready. Thanks to Your work on the cross, Jesus, my journey has already begun. Praise You for giving me a heavenly passport, Lord. Amen.

But our citizenship is in heaven. And we eagerly await a Savior from there, the Lord Jesus Christ.
PHILIPPIANS 3:20 NIV

DAY 231
My Inheritance

I'm beginning to understand what it feels like, Father, to have an inheritance, one that truly matters. Through Your Son, You've given me the hope, the assurance of heaven. Wow, what a gift! Any worldly inheritance would eventually run out, but the one You have in store for me will last forever. No rust will corrode it. No moths will consume it. No thief can steal it. My inheritance is secure in You, Father. What joy to have such a loving Father. Amen.

Praise be to the God and Father of our Lord Jesus Christ! In his great mercy he has given us new birth into a living hope through the resurrection of Jesus Christ from the dead, and into an inheritance that can never perish, spoil or fade. This inheritance is kept in heaven for you.

1 PETER 1:3–4 NIV

DAY 232
Mysteries Revealed

I love a good mystery, Lord, but not always when I'm the one who's mystified or confused. When it comes to my life and my future, I want to see where I'm headed. But my life is like a great novel, isn't it, Father? There are whodunits all over the place! And only You know where the story will take me next. I will do my best to calm my heart as Your great mysteries are revealed, step by step. I'll try not to panic when the twists and turns are darkened by night skies. I'll keep my focus on You, Lord. I know You will never fail me. You have revelations aplenty coming my way. What an adventure! Amen.

*"He reveals the deep things of darkness
and brings utter darkness into the light."*
JOB 12:22 NIV

DAY 233
Greater than My Heart

Sometimes I'm wracked with guilt, Lord. I'm not talking about conviction—I'm talking about full-out can't-sleep, can't-eat, can't-think guilt. I have such a hard time taking steps forward because my feet are stuck in the muck and mire of what I've done. Thank You for the promise that You can (and do) set my heart at rest. You are greater than my heart. What a relief! My heart is heavy, burdened. Today I give it (and this guilt) to You, Father. Forgive me for the wrongs I've done, and ease the weight so that I can begin to move into a bright future with You. Amen.

This is how we know that we belong to the truth
and how we set our hearts at rest in his presence:
If our hearts condemn us, we know that God is
greater than our hearts, and he knows everything.
1 John 3:19–20 niv

DAY 234
What Tomorrow Brings

I'm such a planner, Lord. I know You know this. You see my lists. You know the motivations of my heart. Truth is, I don't know what tomorrow will bring. I can plan all I like, but my future is wholly in Your hands. Today I submit myself to Your will—not just for today but all the days to come. Remind me daily that You are in control, not me. And may I never forget that Your idea of a bright tomorrow is far greater than my own. I can trust You, Lord. Amen.

Come now, you who say, "Today or tomorrow we will go into such and such a town and spend a year there and trade and make a profit"—yet you do not know what tomorrow will bring. What is your life? For you are a mist that appears for a little time and then vanishes. Instead you ought to say, "If the Lord wills, we will live and do this or that."

JAMES 4:13–15 ESV

DAY 235
You Establish My Steps

Father, my very steps are ordered. I can't see the footprints that You've laid out for me, but You can, and even at this very moment, You're guiding me to walk paths set before me. If I get off course, Lord, lead me back. I want to walk confidently into the future, knowing that my direction is set and my course sure. How deep and abiding my trust in You is as I think that through. Amen.

The heart of man plans his way,
but the LORD establishes his steps.
PROVERBS 16:9 ESV

DAY 236
Surely There Is a Future

I love the word *surely*, Lord. For surely there is a future. It's solid. It's set in stone. It's immovable. I can't see it yet, but that's where the adventure begins. My inability to see means that I have no choice but to "let go and let God," as the old saying goes. So that's what I choose today. And I do so, Father, with the assurance that surely there is a future for me, one You've already got mapped out to a T. What hope this brings, what joy! Thank You, Lord, for the "surelys" in my life. Amen.

Surely there is a future,
and your hope will not be cut off.
PROVERBS 23:18 ESV

DAY 237
Every Step of the Way

Lord, I take comfort in the fact that You've made a way of escape for me, even in my darkest hour. If it's true that You have plans for my future, then I have to believe You have a way to escape today's tragedy in order to take me there. No matter how difficult the road ahead, Father, I trust that You will lead me every step of the way. Amen.

The temptations in your life are no different from what others experience. And God is faithful. He will not allow the temptation to be more than you can stand. When you are tempted, he will show you a way out so that you can endure.

1 Corinthians 10:13 nlt

There Will Be a Future

There's a sense of foreboding that hits me sometimes, Father. I feel like my hopes are dashed. There's no future for me. I confess, I often feel like You've overlooked me and are more focused on others. Thank You for the assurance in Your Word that there will be a future for me. I understand my role, Lord: I'm to see wisdom in my soul (my heart and mind). Though this isn't always easy, I will give it my best shot and trust You with the rest. Amen.

Why, my soul, are you downcast? Why so disturbed within me? Put your hope in God, for I will yet praise him, my Savior and my God.

PSALM 42:5 NIV

DAY 239

Nothing Can Separate Me from Your Love

I am loved by You today, Lord, and I will be loved tomorrow. Nothing I do, nothing that happens to me, nothing I go through will ever bring an end to Your amazing adoration for me. Because I know Your love will remain, I can trust that it will drive You as Your plans for my life move forward. What peace this brings, Father. Thank You. Amen.

I am convinced that nothing can ever separate us from God's love. Neither death nor life, neither angels nor demons, neither our fears for today nor our worries about tomorrow—not even the powers of hell can separate us from God's love. No power in the sky above or in the earth below—indeed, nothing in all creation will ever be able to separate us from the love of God that is revealed in Christ Jesus our Lord.
ROMANS 8:38–39 NLT

DAY 240
A Sure and Steadfast Anchor

Strong winds have blown in my life, Lord. Many times, I've wondered if they would toss me overboard. It's comforting to know that You're an anchor in the time of storms. You're sure. You're steadfast. You'll keep me locked in place, standing upright. Because I know I have this anchor, hope stirs in my soul. It's not a false hope, something I drum up in the moment, but a deep, abiding faith that squelches any fears and gives me courage to keep going. Today I choose to cling to You, my immovable, steadfast Father. Thank You for holding all things together. Amen.

We have this as a sure and steadfast anchor of the soul, a hope that enters into the inner place behind the curtain.
HEBREWS 6:19 ESV

DAY 241
Heirs According to the Hope

Wow, I love the idea of an inheritance, Lord! It's an amazing feeling to know you're so special to someone that they've left you something wonderful. You, Father, have left the most amazing gift of all—eternal life. I won't need to wait for lawyers to dole it out either. It's available, starting now. It's Your grace that makes this possible. (And trust me, I've needed that grace so many times.) You've somehow made my crooked life straight again. In spite of my mess-ups, You've kept me in the will, Lord. What an amazing Father You are. I praise You. Amen.

Because of his grace he made us right in his sight and gave us confidence that we will inherit eternal life.

TITUS 3:7 NLT

DAY 242
A Future Hope

Mmm. . .honey. There are so many references to the luscious treat in Your Word, Lord, and I can see why. It adds sweetness to everything it touches. What a revelation, to see that wisdom is like honey. When I approach life's challenges with the wisdom that only You can give, situations are immediately sweetened. And when my situation improves, I'm far more likely to be hopeful about my future. Thank You for the reminder that You've got sweet things in store for me, Father. They're being poured out, even now, like honey for my soul. Now that's a precious promise! I praise You, Lord. Amen.

Know also that wisdom is like honey for you:
If you find it, there is a future hope for you,
and your hope will not be cut off.
PROVERBS 24:14 NIV

DAY 243
That We Might Have Hope

Sometimes I feel like You're a teacher at the blackboard, Lord, scribbling out reminders of things I've forgotten. (How quickly I walk away from Your Word and forget!) You write the words *endurance* and *instruction* on the board, and I am reminded that this race was never meant to be swift or easy. Then I see words like *encouragement* and *hope*, and I realize You've had the answer to my angst all along. Keep my eyes riveted to Your Word, Lord, that I might have hope. You took the time to make sure those blessed words were written down for my instruction. Thank You for that, Lord. Amen.

For whatever was written in former days was written for our instruction, that through endurance and through the encouragement of the Scriptures we might have hope.
ROMANS 15:4 ESV

DAY 244
What I Cannot See

This world offers far too many visual images, Lord, and I'm having a hard time filtering them. All I have to do is turn on the news to instantaneously see tragedies happening all over the world. I can watch with my own eyes as hurricanes rip apart towns, as people rise up in anger against one another, as nations are toppled. It's almost too much to take. Instead of fretting over what I can see, please help me to have hope, based on what I can't see. You're in charge. You've got this. Your plans are mighty to save. Today I choose to hope for what I do not see, and I will wait patiently as Your will is done. Amen.

For in this hope we were saved. Now hope that is seen is not hope. For who hopes for what he sees? But if we hope for what we do not see, we wait for it with patience.
ROMANS 8:24–25 ESV

DAY 245
The Beauty of the Lord

May my pursuit of You, Lord, be my "one thing." May I praise You and serve You in this life, which is but training camp for eternity! I look forward to heaven, Father, where I may truly know the depths of Your beauty. I see glimpses of Your beauty in Your creation. One day it will be fully revealed. What a glorious day that will be! Until then, be my "one thing." I love You, Lord. Amen.

One thing have I desired of the LORD, that will I seek after; that I may dwell in the house of the LORD all the days of my life, to behold the beauty of the LORD, and to enquire in his temple.

PSALM 27:4 KJV

DAY 246
Hope for the Future

Lord, I can't see the future. I see only one piece of the puzzle at a time, but You see the finished product. As I go through this day, I will not fear because You are in control. When things seem hopeless, there is hope. My hope is in a sovereign God who says He knows the plans He has for me. I am counting on You to see me through. Amen.

For I know the thoughts that I think toward you,
saith the LORD, thoughts of peace, and not
of evil, to give you an expected end.
JEREMIAH 29:11 KJV

DAY 247
Serious Warning

Everywhere I look, Father, my society says it's okay. Sex before marriage and outside of marriage. You warn us that this type of sin is of a serious nature. What we do with our bodies stays in our hearts and minds for a very long time. Protect me from the influences in my life that say these things are permissible when Your Word clearly states they are not good for me. Amen.

Flee fornication. Every sin that a man doeth
is without the body; but he that committeth
fornication sinneth against his own body.

1 CORINTHIANS 6:18 KJV

DAY 248
A Load of Stress

Deadlines, sports schedules, unexpected overnight company—I'm about to pull out my hair! I know we all have our share of stress, but didn't I get an extra load this week, Father? I'm not sure what the purpose of it is, but I know there's a reason. Lord, give me patience through the ordeal, and let me please You. Amen.

Take my yoke upon you, and learn of me; for I am meek and lowly in heart: and ye shall find rest unto your souls. For my yoke is easy, and my burden is light.
MATTHEW 11:29–30 KJV

DAY 249
My Source of Strength

Father, at times I worry too much about what others think of me. Even when I just have a minor disagreement with a friend or coworker, I am afraid that the person will not like me anymore. I worry that I have not lived up to what was expected of me. Remind me, Father, that I must seek my ultimate strength and encouragement from You and You alone. Amen.

And David was greatly distressed; for the people spake of stoning him, because the soul of all the people was grieved, every man for his sons and for his daughters: but David encouraged himself in the LORD his God.

1 SAMUEL 30:6 KJV

DAY 250
God's Wisdom

I'm so forgetful! God, I know how many times You've admonished me to seek Your wisdom, yet over and over I try to do things on my own. You'd think I would learn after so many mistakes, but I guess I'm too proud. I don't want to continue like this. I want Your wisdom so that I can live life as You intended. Amen.

O the depth of the riches both of the wisdom and knowledge of God!
ROMANS 11:33 KJV

DAY 251

Prioritizing

Father, I really have a lot to do, and I'm not very good at multitasking. I need Your help each day as I organize the chores that need to be done. Show me how to prioritize my workload so that I can get things done in the most efficient manner, and let my work be pleasing in Your sight. Amen.

But seek ye first the kingdom of God, and his righteousness; and all these things shall be added unto you.

MATTHEW 6:33 KJV

DAY 252
Following Christ's Example

Lord, You are always there, and You are consistently patient with me. What if it were not so? What if You reached Your limit and showed the wrath that I deserve in my sinful imperfection? Because of Your great patience with me, let me not grow tired of being patient myself. Let me model what You have shown me by Your example. Thank You for Your great patience with me, God. Amen.

And let us not be weary in well doing:
for in due season we shall reap, if we faint not.
GALATIANS 6:9 KJV

Come to Jesus

I come to You, Lord Jesus. That is the first step. I come before You now in this quiet moment. As I begin this new day, calm my spirit. There is work that must be done today. But even as I work, I can find rest in You. Ease the tension and stress in me, Lord, as only You can do. Thank You for a sense of peace. Amen.

Come unto me, all ye that labour and are heavy laden, and I will give you rest.
MATTHEW 11:28 KJV

DAY 254
Enjoyable Work

I'm blessed to have a job I enjoy, Lord. So many people aren't able to say the same, and many of them probably have good reason to dislike their work. Thank You for opening this door of opportunity for me. You've met my needs in a wonderful way. Amen.

Not with eyeservice, as menpleasers; but as the servants of Christ, doing the will of God from the heart; with good will doing service, as to the Lord, and not to men.
EPHESIANS 6:6–7 KJV

DAY 255
Trust in His Guidance

Father, this morning I come before You and I praise You. You are good and loving. You have only my very best interests at heart. Take my hand and lead me. Show me the way to go. Like a child being carried in a loving parent's arms, let me relax and trust You. I know that You will never lead me astray. Thank You, God, for this assurance. Amen.

Cause me to hear thy lovingkindness in the morning;
for in thee do I trust: cause me to know the way wherein
I should walk; for I lift up my soul unto thee.

PSALM 143:8 KJV

DAY 256
Joy in the Name of the Lord

Father, this morning I meet You here for just a few moments before the busyness of the day takes over. I trust You. It is not always easy to trust, but You have proven trustworthy in my life. I find joy in the knowledge that You are my defender. You go before me this day into battle. I choose joy today because I love the name of the Lord Almighty. Amen.

*But let all those that put their trust in thee rejoice:
let them ever shout for joy, because thou defendest them:
let them also that love thy name be joyful in thee.*

PSALM 5:11 KJV

DAY 257
Never Really Alone

Heavenly Father, I'm lonely today. There is no one with whom I can share what is going on in my life right now. Oh, I have friends, but no one who would really understand this. But You created me, and You know me like no one else. I ask You today to let me feel Your presence with me. It's a terrible thing to be alone, but You promised You'd never leave. So I know You are with me. I'm grateful for Your constant love and care. In Jesus' name, amen.

God has said, "Never will I leave you;
never will I forsake you."
HEBREWS 13:5 NIV

DAY 258
Up from the Grave

Hope is a living, breathing thing. I see that now, Lord. I'd always pictured it as a word. A choice. A lifeless thing. But it's not. It's very much alive, quickening my heart even now. Hope boosts the adrenaline. Hope steadies my breathing. Hope shifts my focus. Hope keeps my feet moving. And this hope is alive in me because of the resurrection of Your Son, Jesus. Amazing! When He rose from the dead, He set in motion a hope that refuses to die. What an amazing, motivational gift, Father. Praise You for this hope. Amen.

Through him you believe in God, who raised
him from the dead and glorified him, and
so your faith and hope are in God.

1 PETER 1:21 NIV

DAY 259
Boasting in Our Hope

Now, this is one time I don't mind boasting, Lord! I love to brag on You. When other people ask me how I keep going, why I don't crater, I tell them the reason for my hope: You. I sing Your praises. It doesn't always make sense to others, but I love sharing how You're growing me into someone different than I used to be. Watching how I persevere is giving others hope, Father. Your hope will never put me to shame. I praise You for the hope You've placed in my heart, Lord. I'm bragging on You today. Amen.

And we boast in the hope of the glory of God. Not only so, but we also glory in our sufferings, because we know that suffering produces perseverance; perseverance, character; and character, hope. And hope does not put us to shame, because God's love has been poured out into our hearts through the Holy Spirit, who has been given to us.

ROMANS 5:2–5 NIV

DAY 260
Because There Is Hope

I love the word *secure*, Lord. This world is anything but! I'm forced to lock my doors day and night. I get nervous sending my kids or grandkids off to school. There's so much to make me anxious. But in You, Father, I place my trust. In You, we all have security beyond anything the world can offer. We don't have to live in fear. Please replace those fears with hope today, Lord. When I put my head on my pillow at night, I want to rest secure in You. Do a work in my heart and mind, I pray. Amen.

"You will be secure, because there is hope; you will look about you and take your rest in safety."

JOB 11:18 NIV

DAY 261
A Hope That's Wanted

This is a hard thing to admit, Lord, but sometimes I simply give up hoping. I don't even want to try anymore because I'm afraid I'll be let down. I can relate to the crippled man in today's scripture. He'd been waiting a long time and probably felt his turn would never come. But when Jesus stepped onto the scene, everything changed. I ask You to renew my hope today, Lord. Give me the desire for change. When You ask, "Do you really want this?" I want to be able to answer with a resounding, "Yes, Lord!" Only You can bring about the necessary changes in my heart, Father. Today I give You permission to do just that. Amen.

When Jesus saw him lying there and learned that
he had been in this condition for a long time,
he asked him, "Do you want to get well?"

JOHN 5:6 NIV

DAY 262
A Seed of Hope

I love this image of the mustard seed, Father. It's so small, yet it produces one of the largest spices. So many times I feel like my faith is tiny, like that little seed. But You are capable of taking something so small and growing it exponentially. Watching this amazing growth causes hope to grow too. Today I give You my mustard-seed faith. Take it, Lord, and breathe on it, that transformation might take place. Amen.

Jesus said, "In what way can we show what the holy nation of God is like? Or what picture-story can we use to help you understand? It is like a grain of mustard seed that is planted in the ground. It is the smallest of all seeds. After it is put in the ground, it grows and becomes the largest of the spices. It puts out long branches so birds of the sky can live in it."

MARK 4:30–32 NLV

DAY 263
A Shield around Me

I hear what they're saying, Lord. They're pointing fingers and whispering, "She won't make it this time. She's going under." Oh, if only they could see what I'm seeing! You have hemmed me in on every side, giving me refuge, even in the midst of troubles. I'm not afraid when I see the efforts You're putting forth to keep me safe. You're like an impenetrable shield all around me. Let those arrows fling. They won't hit me as long as You're on my side. What hope this brings, Father. What confidence. Today I choose to trust in You. Amen.

Many are saying of me, "God will not deliver him."
But you, LORD, are a shield around me, my glory, the
One who lifts my head high. I call out to the Lord, and he
answers me from his holy mountain. I lie down and sleep;
I wake again, because the Lord sustains me. I will not fear
though tens of thousands assail me on every side.

PSALM 3:2–6 NIV

DAY 264
Overflowing with Hope

What a day that must have been, Lord, when water gushed from a rock! I love this picture because it reminds me that You can make living water out of even the hardest situation in my life. With one tap from You, life flows. If the Israelites could trust You to provide water in the desert, surely I can trust You to supply my daily needs. My hope is restored as I see how diligent You care for even the tiniest details. Thank You for Your provision, Lord, and this amazing story of hope. I praise You. Amen.

"He struck the rock so that water gushed out and streams overflowed. Can he also give bread or provide meat for his people?"
PSALM 78:20 ESV

DAY 265
The Reason for My Hope

I'm so excited that You are motivated to move on my behalf, Lord. Your Word says I need to be ready to explain the reason for my hope, which tells me that You care a great deal about breathing life into my situations. When people rise up against me, I won't be afraid. I'll be ready to give an answer to naysayers, knowing that You're going to move on my behalf. May others be motivated by this hope inside me. I want to be a good witness for You, Lord. Amen.

But in your hearts revere Christ as Lord. Always be prepared to give an answer to everyone who asks you to give the reason for the hope that you have. But do this with gentleness and respect, keeping a clear conscience, so that those who speak maliciously against your good behavior in Christ may be ashamed of their slander.

1 PETER 3:15–16 NIV

DAY 266
Peace Is My Guard

I'm so fickle, Lord. My emotions go up and down as life's circumstances present challenges that seem too much to bear. I'm not proud of this, but when I'm running on empty (or when my peace is waning) it's easy to get caught up in the emotions and lose heart. Thank You for the reminder that Your peace transcends understanding. I don't have to "get it" to be peaceful. I can experience peace even when the storm rages around me. What a revelation, to read that Your peace serves as a guard around my heart. Wow! May it shift my focus to You, that I might live this way, all of my days. Amen.

And the peace of God, which transcends all understanding, will guard your hearts and your minds in Christ Jesus.

PHILIPPIANS 4:7 NIV

DAY 267
My Thought Life Matters

When my hope is waning, remind me of this verse, Lord. My thoughts always lead to actions (good or bad), so keep my thoughts on the things that please You. I want to focus on things that are true, not the deceptions of this world or the lies I hear from those who don't know You. I need to focus on noble things—like caring for the poor, tending to those in need. Help me shift my thoughts to doing the right things and remaining pure (a task that isn't always easy in today's society). Lord, may all of my focus be on admirable, lovely things, and may I be a reflection of You to a watching world. Amen.

Finally, brothers and sisters, whatever is true, whatever is noble, whatever is right, whatever is pure, whatever is lovely, whatever is admirable—if anything is excellent or praiseworthy—think about such things.
PHILIPPIANS 4:8 NIV

DAY 268
You Are Rejoicing over Me

How could I remain in the pits when I read a verse like this? I can picture You now, Lord, singing and dancing over me in celebratory fashion. I can imagine the delight on Your face as I learn and grow, as I'm transformed into Your image. It's the same expression I have when I see a toddler making new discoveries or choosing to obey his parents. You're a proud Papa, a Daddy who longs to sweep His daughter into His arms for a spin around the dance floor. What a blessed daughter I am too. I'm so happy to bring a smile to Your face. Carry on with the song, Lord—may it spill over into my heart too! Amen.

"The LORD your God is with you, the Mighty Warrior who saves. He will take great delight in you; in his love he will no longer rebuke you, but will rejoice over you with singing."

ZEPHANIAH 3:17 NIV

DAY 269
Anger

God, I need a solution for my anger. Sometimes I let it take over then end up regretting what it leads me to say or do. As I pray and study and grow closer to You, show me ways to control it. Guide me to the right verses to memorize and incorporate into my life. Lead me to someone who can keep me accountable. And, most of all, help me strive for self-control. Amen.

If it is possible, as much as depends on you,
live peaceably with all men. Beloved, do not avenge
yourselves, but rather give place to wrath; for it is
written, "Vengeance is Mine, I will repay," says the Lord.
ROMANS 12:18–19 NKJV

DAY 270
A Friendlier World

Dear God, I was just noticing all the people around me who really could use a friend. For whatever reason, they're alone and hurting. I need to reach out to them. I ask You to give me opportunities and ideas to let them know I care. Let me make the world a little friendlier for them. Amen.

Finally, be ye all of one mind, having compassion one of another, love as brethren, be pitiful, be courteous.
1 PETER 3:8 KJV

DAY 271
Tears

I've heard, God, that tears speak their own language. If that's true, then You made women verbal in two ways— words and tears. Being the gentler, more emotional reflection of Your image, we tend to cry easily. Like most women, I cry for a variety of reasons, and sometimes for no reason at all, like today. But since You read what's in my heart, I know You understand. Thank You for valuing my tears. Amen.

Put my tears into Your bottle;
are they not in Your book?
PSALM 56:8 NKJV

DAY 272
Power Boost

Dear God, please help me hold together the pieces of my life. My to-do list seems endless. There is always someone needing me. There are constant demands on my energy and sanity. I feel like I go through life in a state of exhaustion. I know that keeps me from being at my peak. And I know You want me to care for my health. But I'm stuck in a cycle of busyness that has no end in sight. Show me what I can change, Lord. Show me how to get the emotional and physical wellness I need. Amen.

He gives power to the weak, and to those who have no might He increases strength. . . . Those who wait on the LORD shall renew their strength; they shall mount up with wings like eagles, they shall run and not be weary, they shall walk and not faint.
ISAIAH 40:29, 31 NKJV

DAY 273
Delicate, Powerful Faith

God, faith is such a delicate concept, yet so mighty in its power. Faith isn't something I can wrap my arms around, but it is something I can rest my soul in. Hebrews 11:1 says it's "the evidence of things not seen." That means it's like a virtual item—something that already exists, though you can't hold it in your hand. Faith is sometimes trivialized in our world, but it is of utmost importance to You. Please increase my faith, O Lord. In Christ's name, amen.

Now faith is the substance of things hoped for,
the evidence of things not seen.

HEBREWS 11:1 KJV

DAY 274
Christ's Loneliness

Lord, how alone You must have been in the garden when the disciples fell asleep. And when God turned His back as You hung on the cross—was there anything to compare to what You felt? Yet You did it willingly. You understand when I'm lonely, and I thank You for being there during those times. Amen.

Fear thou not; for I am with thee: be not dismayed;
for I am thy God: I will strengthen thee; yea,
I will help thee; yea, I will uphold thee with
the right hand of my righteousness.

ISAIAH 41:10 KJV

DAY 275
Granting Forgiveness

Heavenly Father, I need to forgive someone who wronged me. I know it's the right thing, but it's so difficult. I can't do it in my own strength. Give me the power to extend grace to this person. Put Your love in my heart so I can have a gracious attitude and heart of mercy. The Bible tells me to forgive because I have been forgiven. This is my chance to put it into practice. I'm leaning on Your power. In Jesus' name, amen.

"And whenever you stand praying, if you have anything against anyone, forgive him, that your Father in heaven may also forgive you your trespasses."

MARK 11:25 NKJV

DAY 276
Criticism and Judging

Dear Lord, criticism can be so hurtful. It's easy to give, but so difficult to receive. Sometimes people paraphrase Matthew 7:1 as "Don't judge." But it actually means "Don't judge unless you want to be judged." I don't think we realize that when we criticize others, we open ourselves up to the same kind of scrutiny. I'm not very good at living up to this standard. Help me to be less critical of others. Check me, Holy Spirit, when I start to say something judgmental. Amen.

Set a guard over my mouth, LORD;
keep watch over the door of my lips.
PSALM 141:3 NIV

DAY 277
Family Time

Thank You for my home, dear Jesus. I just love to be here. I can't explain the joy that comes from being surrounded by those I love. Whether our home is filled with laughter during game night or shrouded in silent contemplation during family devotions, I can feel Your presence, and I am uplifted. Amen.

Be kindly affectioned one to another with brotherly love; in honour preferring one another.
ROMANS 12:10 KJV

DAY 278
Endurance Required

I'm finding, Lord, that the Christian life is one that requires endurance. It isn't enough to start well. So let me patiently and steadily move down the road to Christlikeness. I know difficulties will come; I've faced some already. It reminds me of the words of the second verse of "Amazing Grace": "Through many dangers, toils and snares, I have already come. 'Tis grace that brought me safe thus far, and grace will lead me home." In Your name, amen.

Let us run with endurance the race that is set before us.

Hebrews 12:1 nkjv

DAY 279
To-Do Lists

God, I like to know what's coming up next in my life. I like to chart the items requiring some kind of action from me. To-do lists are my way of planning out the day and week. The lists keep me on track, but anything can be detrimental if it becomes too important. Help me not to plot and plan my life so completely that there is no room for divine interruptions, for Providence to intervene. Give me patience with those who cause my day to go awry; let me see beyond the irritation to what You have in mind. In Jesus' name, amen.

We can make our plans, but the
LORD determines our steps.
PROVERBS 16:9 NLT

DAY 280
Filled with Love

Lord, let my home be a comforting haven for my family and friends. May it be a place where they can momentarily escape the pressures of this world. Help me to do my best to make it a place where people will know they are loved by me and, more importantly, by You. Amen.

A new commandment I give unto you,
that ye love one another; as I have loved
you, that ye also love one another.

JOHN 13:34 KJV

DAY 281
Deep Surrender

Lord, I need to surrender to You. You've shown me an area of my life that I've been trying to rule. I know You need the keys to every room in my heart, and so here I am, bringing this one to You. Surrender means I give You permission to change, clean out, and add things. Waving the white flag isn't really easy, but it's the way to true joy. Thank You for showing me that. Amen.

But now, O Lord, You are our Father;
we are the clay, and You our potter;
and all we are the work of Your hand.

ISAIAH 64:8 NKJV

DAY 282
Trust in His Strength

Lord, at times I get cocky. I step out on my own and think I've got everything under control. But then something happens that shakes my world. I find myself calling on You and hoping You will come. You always show up. You always remember me. I am Your child. Help me to trust You before I am desperate. Help me to remember the source of my strength. Amen.

For I will not trust in my bow,
neither shall my sword save me.
PSALM 44:6 KJV

DAY 283
The Heart of Giving

Jesus, You see the heart of the giver. I can imagine the shock of the disciples when You declared the widow's small gift greater than that of the rich. They gave of their excess. She gave all she had. She wanted to be part of the kingdom work. She trusted You to meet her needs. May I have a true giver's heart. May I give sacrificially as the widow did that day. Amen.

Verily I say unto you, That this poor widow hath cast more in, than all they which have cast into the treasury: for all they did cast in of their abundance; but she of her want did cast in all that she had, even all her living.

MARK 12:43–44 KJV

DAY 284
The Center of God's Will

Lord, I know that in the center of Your will are peace, joy, and many other rich blessings. I'd like to experience all these things, but the trouble I seem to have is figuring out what Your will is for me. Please help me be attentive when You speak, and give me a heart willing to be used by You. Amen.

Commit thy works unto the LORD,
and thy thoughts shall be established.
PROVERBS 16:3 KJV

DAY 285
Saved by Grace through Faith

God, it is so comforting to know that my position before You is secure. Thank You for seeing me through a new lens. When You look at me, because I have been saved through faith, You see Your Son in me. You no longer see sin but righteousness. I couldn't have earned it, no matter how hard I worked. Thank You for the gift of salvation through my faith in Jesus. Amen.

For by grace are ye saved through faith;
and that not of yourselves: it is the gift of God:
not of works, lest any man should boast.
Ephesians 2:8–9 kjv

DAY 286
Resting on the Sabbath

Father, You created us as beings who work and need rest. Sometimes I forget that. I get so caught up in all that must be accomplished. Slow my pace, Lord. Help me to honor You by resting one day per week. Help me to keep the Sabbath holy. Thank You for designing the week and for telling Your people to rest. It is up to me to follow Your command. Amen.

Remember the sabbath day, to keep it holy.
Six days shalt thou labour, and do all thy work:
but the seventh day is the sabbath of the LORD
thy God: in it thou shalt not do any work.
EXODUS 20:8–10 KJV

DAY 287
Being Godly on Purpose

Lord, I was recently reminded that godly character doesn't just happen. I have to purpose in my heart to live a life pleasing to You. Only then will I be able to stand strong when peer pressure threatens to undo me. I want to commit daily to obeying You. Amen.

And be not conformed to this world: but be ye transformed by the renewing of your mind, that ye may prove what is that good, and acceptable, and perfect, will of God.
ROMANS 12:2 KJV

DAY 288
God Is Faithful

God, I focus a lot on my faith in You. And then You show me that it is not all about me. You are faithful to me. You show me how to be faithful. You never leave. You never give up on me. You never turn away. You always show up. You always believe in me. You are faithful by Your very nature. You cannot be unfaithful. Thank You for Your faithfulness in my life. Amen.

But the Lord is faithful, who shall stablish you, and keep you from evil.
2 Thessalonians 3:3 kjv

DAY 289
You Hear. . .and Act

Are You waiting right now, Lord? Waiting for me to pack away my pride, turn to You, and seek Your face? Are You waiting for Your people to turn from the things that have bound them, to cry out to You, and to ask for forgiveness of sins? I can't even imagine what it must feel like on Your end, Lord, as You wait for Your children to do the right thing. You're such a gracious God! The minute You hear our call, You spring into action. And You don't stop there. You're so motivated by our call that You forgive our sin and bring healing to our land. Father, forgive me for the many times I've kept You waiting. I turn to You today. Amen.

*"If My people who are called by My name put away
their pride and pray, and look for My face, and turn
from their sinful ways, then I will hear from heaven.
I will forgive their sin, and will heal their land."*
2 Chronicles 7:14 nlv

DAY 290
Shining-Greatness Is on Its Way

I'm trying to imagine what Your shining-greatness will look like, Lord. I've already tasted of Your goodness, shared in Your blessings, and witnessed miracles. I've spent quiet, intimate time in Your presence and have marveled that You continue to woo someone as flawed as me. There's really more to come, Lord? I can hardly wait. When I'm in the middle of a rough patch, please remind me that my suffering is only temporary. It cannot be compared with the glory around the bend, Father. I can only imagine what You've got in store. Praise You! Amen.

I am sure that our suffering now cannot be compared to the shining-greatness that He is going to give us.

ROMANS 8:18 NLV

DAY 291
You Know My Path

Not everyone is for me. I know this, Lord. There are people who would rather not see me succeed. They want to
knock me off my path, but I won't let them get me down,
or send me veering in the wrong direction. Even when
they weaken my resistance, I'll keep my focus on You.
You're the only one who knows the direction this road is
leading. How could I help but trust You? No matter how
many traps are set, You'll guide me safely past them, so
that I can continue to grow in You. Praise You for that,
Lord. Amen.

When my spirit had grown weak within me,
You knew my path. They have hidden a
trap for me in the way where I walk.

PSALM 142:3 NLV

DAY 292
Your Works Abound

Not a day goes by that I don't marvel at Your creation, Lord. The lustrous blue sky. The curving peaks of a mountain range. An infant's joyous smile. A butterfly, its wings spread in flight. A hummingbird alighting on a feeder. Signs of Your creative handiwork abound. If You took the time to pour such thought into even the smallest of things, then I know You've spent even more effort designing me. And You've designed me for greatness, Father. I pray that my works will abound as well. May I do great and mighty things for Your kingdom, Lord. Amen.

O Lord, how many are Your works! You made them all in wisdom. The earth is full of what You have made.
PSALM 104:24 NLV

DAY 293
You Intercede for Me

Father, I know what it's like to intercede for someone. I've gone to bat for loved ones many times over. When I feel passionately about a situation, I'm happy to come out swinging. It's amazing to me that You search my heart and Your Spirit intercedes for me, according to Your will. Even now, intercession is taking place for millions across this globe as You search hearts from continent to continent. Remarkable! There are things happening in the spiritual realm that we cannot see or hear, but I'm thrilled to know You are for us, not against us. Thank You for caring and for interceding on our behalf. Amen.

He who searches our hearts knows the mind of the Spirit, because the Spirit intercedes for God's people in accordance with the will of God.

ROMANS 8:27 NIV

DAY 294
You Meet My Needs

Okay, I'll confess—this is a tough one for me at times, Lord. Sometimes worries slip in. I wonder about the bills. I question Your ability to provide for me. I get bound up with worry as I see my apparent lack. But with You, Father, there is no lack! Thank You for that reminder. I don't want to run after "stuff." You know what I need, and You'll make sure I have enough for each day. That's Your promise. You'll meet all of my needs—emotional, financial, spiritual, and physical. You've got me covered, Lord, and I'm so grateful. Praise You. Amen.

"So do not worry, saying, 'What shall we eat?' or 'What shall we drink?' or 'What shall we wear?' For the pagans run after all these things, and your heavenly Father knows that you need them."
MATTHEW 6:31–32 NIV

DAY 295
You Bring Me Forth as Gold

I'm beginning to understand the phrase "trial by fire," Lord. It's not fun, going through the fire, but the result is pretty astounding! I'm like a beautiful golden ring, exquisitely shaped by the Master Artist. Best of all, the trial by fire purifies me and rids me of the things that drag me down. Your plans for me are so holy, Lord, so special, that they require me to be the best I can be. So purify my heart today, Father. Cleanse me from within. Shape me into Your image. Bring me from the furnace, a new woman of God, ready to do Your will. I submit myself to the process, Lord. Amen.

"But he knows the way that I take; when he has tested me, I will come forth as gold."

JOB 23:10 NIV

DAY 296
Things Not Seen

Jesus, it is easy to believe in that which I can see. I wish I could reach out and touch You. As I meditate on Your Word, give me faith in that which I cannot see. Give me faith that all of Your promises are true and that one day You will come again in the clouds to take me home. Amen.

Now faith is the substance of things hoped for,
the evidence of things not seen.
HEBREWS 11:1 KJV

DAY 297
Special Instructions

Thank You for Your Word, Father. Without it I would be a helpless cause in regard to developing godly character. I'm so glad You preserved these special words that give me specific instruction on how to live. Help me to hide these scriptures in my heart so that I'm able to rely on them throughout my life. Amen.

Thy word is a lamp unto my feet,
and a light unto my path.
PSALM 119:105 KJV

DAY 298
Poise

Heavenly Father, I need poise—that kind of gracious manner and behavior that characterized women of past generations. It seems to be disdained in my culture. Women now are expected and encouraged to be free spirits—unrestricted by convention and decorum. But I cringe when I observe women using crude language, slouching in their seats, and adopting careless ways of walking and eating. I don't want to seem prissy and uppity, but I do want to guard against being too informal. Help me develop the traits that portray womanhood as the gentle, beautiful, fascinating gender You designed. Amen.

Like a gold ring in a pig's snout is a
beautiful woman who shows no discretion.
PROVERBS 11:22 NIV

DAY 299
Blank Stares

Today I'm struggling, Jesus. I have a specific goal that needs to be met, but it requires clarity of mind. The project is spread out before me, but I'm staring at it blankly. I know You want me to work on it, and I need Your guidance. Give me the ability to think and complete the task. Amen.

In all thy ways acknowledge him,
and he shall direct thy paths.
PROVERBS 3:6 KJV

DAY 300
Food Budgeting

God, I'm really struggling today with self-worth because I just feel so fat. I know I need discipline—to eat less and exercise more. I do pretty well for a while, but then I get off track. And dieting feels like fake living. I mean, who seriously thinks no-fat cheese is delicious? I see skinny people every day who can wear stylish clothing and aren't afraid to stand in the front row when group pictures are taken. I want that kind of freedom, Lord, so help me "budget" my food so I can rid myself of feeling overblown. Amen.

But the fruit of the Spirit is. . .self-control.
GALATIANS 5:22–23 NIV

DAY 301
First Glimpse of Gray

Lord, I found a gray hair today. I guess I could call it silver (not good) or white (even worse). Whatever the tint is, it's not the color I was born with! I realize the aging process is part of the death process and death in our world is the result of sin. So I feel perfectly justified in not wanting to age. But I must acknowledge the fact that I cannot continually stay in the youthful season of life. Please give me whatever kind of grace I need to resist adopting a nasty attitude about growing older, and renew my strength every day. Amen.

Therefore we do not lose heart. Though outwardly
we are wasting away, yet inwardly we
are being renewed day by day.

2 Corinthians 4:16 niv

DAY 302
Consulting Christ

Lord, often in my daily planning I forget to consult You. Then I wonder why things don't work out the way I think they should. Forgive my arrogant attitude. I know that only as You guide me through the day will I find joy in accomplishments. Show me how to align my goals with Your will. Amen.

Trust in the LORD with all thine heart;
and lean not unto thine own understanding.
PROVERBS 3:5 KJV

DAY 303
Hospitality

Dear Lord, I need to improve my skills in hospitality. Because You have blessed me, I need to share with others. In fact, hospitality is one of those virtues the apostle Paul commanded of the church. Sharing my home with others is my Christian duty and also a great way to reach out to unbelievers whom I have befriended. Please let me not dread hosting others but rather find ways to make it doable and enjoyable for all. In Jesus' name, amen.

Use hospitality one to another without grudging.
1 PETER 4:9 KJV

DAY 304
Meekness

Heavenly Father, I want to develop the characteristic of meekness, a kind of quiet strength. Rather than a sign of a pushover, meekness is a trait of the strong. It takes guts to be silent when you want to speak. Meekness is not a goal for the weak of heart. It is, rather, for those who would be in the forefront of spiritual growth. Like Moses, the meekest man on earth (see Numbers 12:3), we can reap the rewards of quiet strength in our lives. Amen.

With all lowliness and meekness, with longsuffering, forbearing one another in love.
EPHESIANS 4:2 KJV

Reached Goals

Sometimes I get a little discouraged, Jesus. I feel like I've reached all the goals I've set for myself and that there's nothing for me to achieve that would bring any excitement. Please give me a new outlook. Give me wisdom as I set new goals, and help me to give You the glory when I succeed. Amen.

For wisdom is better than rubies; and all the things that may be desired are not to be compared to it.

PROVERBS 8:11 KJV

DAY 306
Lord, Carry My Friend

My friend is hurting, dear Jesus. She's had so many struggles in her life lately, and she feels like she's about to hit rock bottom. I've tried to be there for her, but right now she needs You in a special way. Please let her know that You want to carry her through this trial. Help her to trust You. Amen.

A friend loveth at all times.
PROVERBS 17:17 KJV

DAY 307
Blessed Are the Flexible

Flexibility is a struggle for me, God. I don't like interruptions in my routine. It's challenging for me to accept a rerouting of my day. Still, sometimes, You have to reorganize for me, because I haven't recognized Your promptings. Or maybe there's someone You need me to meet or a disaster You want me to avoid. Help me to accept the detours in my plan today, aware of Your sovereignty over all. Amen.

This is the day the LORD has made;
we will rejoice and be glad in it.
PSALM 118:24 NKJV

DAY 308
Cheerfulness

Jesus, I can't imagine You as a sour, solemn man. I believe You enjoyed life immensely, and I know You brought joy to those around You. Why else would "sinners and tax collectors" want to eat with You (as Your enemies pointed out)? Your mission on this planet was sacred and grave; but I believe Your demeanor in everyday life was buoyant and pleasant. Others loved being in Your presence. Help me pattern my daily attitude after Your example and take heed of Your command to "be of good cheer." Let me reflect You by the way I approach living. Amen.

"Be of good cheer, daughter."

MATTHEW 9:22 NKJV

DAY 309
Spiritual Guardrails

Dear God, help me to erect proper boundaries in my life. I don't want to fall prey to a sin simply because I wasn't being careful. Just like guardrails on a dangerous mountain highway, boundaries in my life keep me closer to center and farther away from the cliffs. I know Satan is plotting my destruction, but Your power is greater. Let me cooperate with Your grace by a careful lifestyle and a discerning spirit. In Christ's name, amen.

Stay alert! Watch out for your great enemy, the devil. He prowls around like a roaring lion, looking for someone to devour.

1 PETER 5:8 NLT

DAY 310
Natural Consequences

Dear Lord, I know You've forgiven me for that horrible wrong. I thought when I repented that would take care of things, but I'm learning that the natural consequences still hurt. I know they won't disappear, but I pray that You will use them in a positive way—perhaps to keep others from making the same mistake. Amen.

Blessed is he whose transgression
is forgiven, whose sin is covered.
Psalm 32:1 kjv

DAY 311
Role Reversal

Dear Lord, when I was growing up, my parents seemed ageless. But I realize now that my time with them is getting shorter every day. They're getting older, Lord; and, more and more, I find myself looking out for them. This role reversal is really difficult for me. I'm accustomed to them looking out for me, and part of me wishes I could stay in their care for a while longer. Please give me strength to deal with this new phase of our relationship, and help me to honor them as long as they live and beyond. Amen.

"Even to your old age, I am He, and even to gray hairs
I will carry you! I have made, and I will bear;
even I will carry, and will deliver you."

Isaiah 46:4 nkjv

DAY 312
Keep Me

Dear Father, in the scurry of life, I often forget to be thankful for important things. So many times You've shielded my family from physical harm, and I didn't know it until later. And I'm sure I don't even know about all those moments when You've guarded us from spiritual danger. Although we are the apple of Your eye, I realize we're not immune to trauma and disaster; You won't remove the effects of the curse until the right time comes. But for now, I'm grateful that You care about us and that the only way something can touch us is after it's passed Your gentle inspection. Amen.

Keep me as the apple of the eye,
hide me under the shadow of thy wings.
PSALM 17:8 KJV

A Shining Light

Dear God, I want to be a better witness for You. I have friends and family members who don't know You, and every day I interact with people who aren't believers. Lord, I don't want to be corny or pushy, but I do want to let my light shine before others. I ask You to open up the doors for me today. Let me sense Your prompting. And let the silent witness of my life also speak to others about Your great plan of salvation. In Jesus' name, amen.

"Let your light so shine before men,
that they may see your good works
and glorify your Father in heaven."

MATTHEW 5:16 NKJV

DAY 314
God Is a Shield

Protector God, today I'm remembering someone in the armed forces. Though I know war wasn't in Your original plan for this world, it has become a necessary tool for overcoming evil. The Bible recounts stories of You leading Your people, the Israelites, into battle to defend what was right. So there is honor in defending freedom and justice. I ask You to protect this one from danger; dispatch Your peace, and put a hedge before, behind, and around him. Watch over all those who are putting their lives in harm's way for my sake. In Christ's name, amen.

He shields all who take refuge in him.... He trains my hands for battle; my arms can bend a bow of bronze. You make your saving help my shield.
PSALM 18:30, 34–35 NIV

DAY 315
A Strong Tower

I've scoped out my house, Lord, and know just where to go in case of an emergency. I've picked out the safest room, one where I can wait out the storms. There's another place I love to run to when spiritual storms hit. I sprint straight into Your presence. Not that I have to run very far. You're right next to me, after all. All I have to do is speak the name of Jesus and I'm cocooned in safety. Thank You, my Strong Tower, for always being a refuge. Nothing can harm me when I'm tucked away in that holy place. Praise You, Lord! Amen.

The name of the LORD is a fortified tower;
the righteous run to it and are safe.
PROVERBS 18:10 NIV

DAY 316
A Forever-After Journey

I love looking through a telescope, Lord, to the vast corners of this marvelous universe. It's an amazing thing, to see so far out into space. Oh, but how much farther, to see all the way into eternity. There's no telescope powerful enough. Your Word gives me amazing glimpses though, and what I see gets me excited! You've got such joyous things planned for Your kids when we reach heaven. No tears. No crying. Just a forever-after journey with the King of kings and Lord of lords. Praise You for this amazing gift, Father. I can't wait to spend eternity with You. Amen.

For the wages of sin is death, but the gift of God is eternal life in Christ Jesus our Lord.
ROMANS 6:23 NKJV

DAY 317
Steadfast

Father, this verse reminds me of how I feel when I watch the news during a major storm and see those reporters out in high winds. I'm always terrified they'll blow over! Sometimes I'm afraid I'll blow over too, and not just during stormy seasons. Life's circumstances are overwhelming at times and threaten to take me down. But Your Word tells me that I can be immovable. Those winds won't topple me. I know nothing will bring me harm when I walk in Your strength, Father. Show me how to remain steadfast, even when the storms of life thunder overhead. Amen.

Therefore, my beloved brethren, be steadfast, immovable, always abounding in the work of the Lord, knowing that your labor is not in vain in the Lord.
1 Corinthians 15:58 nkjv

DAY 318
More than I Could Ask or Imagine

I've always loved this verse, Lord! I'm a dreamer with a vivid imagination, as You well know, so I'm always asking for over-the-top things. It's so fun to realize that You are able to do immeasurably more than all I could ask or think. You do it all by Your power, Father, not mine. (This is a very good thing, as I'm limited in my abilities.) Your plans for me include fun, over-the-top things, because You're a creative God. I can't wait to see what You have in store. Looking forward to it, Father. Amen.

Now to him who is able to do immeasurably more than all we ask or imagine, according to his power that is at work within us, to him be glory in the church and in Christ Jesus throughout all generations, for ever and ever! Amen.
Ephesians 3:20–21 niv

DAY 319
Lost!

Lord, I've lost my cell phone again! Please help me find it! I know sometimes I'm careless; help me learn from this. But, Lord, You know how much information is in that phone and how much I need it to carry out my responsibilities today. You know where it is right now. Help me think of that place. Guide me to it. And just like the woman with the lost coin—I will rejoice! Amen.

*"Rejoice with me, for I have
found the piece which I lost!"*
LUKE 15:9 NKJV

DAY 320
Wise Fear

"The fear of the LORD is the beginning of wisdom" (Psalm 111:10). Sometimes this passage from Your Word seems almost contradictory, Lord. But there is healthy fear, and then there's crippling fear. I know this passage means that my respect of You is so deep that I abhor sin. Please help me to have this wise fear. Amen.

The fear of the LORD is the beginning of wisdom:
and the knowledge of the holy is understanding.

PROVERBS 9:10 KJV

DAY 321
Difficult People

Dear Lord, I ask You to help me be patient and kind today. The Bible speaks about long-suffering. That's what I need as I deal with difficult people and irritating situations. Whether it's squabbling children or rude drivers or harried clerks, I know there will be those today who will irk me. In those moments when I want to scream, help me remember to forbear and forgive. It's just so easy to react, but help me instead to deliberately choose my response. I'm depending on Your power, Father. Amen.

Bear with each other and forgive one another if any of you has a grievance against someone.
COLOSSIANS 3:13 NIV

DAY 322
Getting Started

Dear Lord, the first step toward any goal is the hardest, and I just don't feel motivated to take it. But there are things I need to do, and so far I haven't found a fairy to do them for me. Procrastination is a terrible hindrance. I know. I'm a closet procrastinator. I don't like to admit to it, but You see it anyway. Thank You for giving me more chances than I deserve. Remind me that I just need to start. Inspiration often springs from soil watered with obedience. Let me learn this lesson well. Amen.

The way of the sluggard is blocked with thorns.
PROVERBS 15:19 NIV

DAY 323
Strength to Stand

Lord, as large as my family is, there are bound to be some members whose life views are significantly different from mine. At times this gets annoying, particularly when they attempt to force their outlook on me. Give me the strength to stand for what I know to be true, and help me to love my family despite our differences. In Jesus' name, amen.

In the day when I cried thou answeredst me,
and strengthenedst me with strength in my soul.
PSALM 138:3 KJV

DAY 324
Slice of Life

Dear Lord, the transition of minutes to hours is so incremental that it is tedious to observe. It's much easier to focus on large chunks of time than myriad tiny ones. Yet hours are made up of minutes, just like the body is comprised of cells. Each is vital to the whole. Lord, help me remember that each minute of the day is a small section, a slice of my life. Help me make the best use of every minute. Amen.

Use every chance you have for doing good,
because these are evil times.
EPHESIANS 5:16 NCV

DAY 325
Internal Clocks

Heavenly Father, it seems like every person has an internal rhythm seemingly permanently set to a certain time of the day. There are early birds and night owls and middle-of-the-day people. Not many of us are successful in changing our internal clock, Lord. Maybe You wanted to create humans with varying peak hours of energy. It would be a pretty boring world if we all fizzled out at the same time each day. Thank You for the variety You have provided in all of us. Amen.

To declare Your lovingkindness in the morning,
and Your faithfulness every night.
PSALM 92:2 NKJV

DAY 326
Filled with Contentment

Sometimes my attitude is so "poor me" that I even get sick, Father. I keep thinking that if only I could have this or that, life would be easier. I know I'm missing out on a truly abundant life by whining so much, and I ask You to forgive me. Fill me with contentment. Amen.

Not that I speak in respect of want: for I have learned,
in whatsoever state I am, therewith to be content.
PHILIPPIANS 4:11 KJV

DAY 327
A Father

God, help me remember that You're my Father. A heavenly Father—One who has unlimited resources and power and One who has infinitely more love than any great earthly dad. When Satan tempts me to view You with suspicion, help me remember that his goal is my utter destruction. Lord, fill my heart with the truth that You love me perfectly and have only the best in mind for me. In fact, You want to embrace me, bless me, and give me heaven as my inheritance. What a wonderful Father You are! Amen.

As a father has compassion on his children, so the LORD has compassion on those who fear him.

PSALM 103:13 NIV

DAY 328
The Gift of Salvation

Dear Father, thank You for the gift of salvation, for sending Your only Son to be a sacrifice for all people, even those who didn't want Him. I am in awe of Your mercy extended to me. It is incredible to think that I am a daughter of God. Thank You, Jesus: You didn't walk away from the cross, but You laid down Your life for me. Thank You, Holy Spirit, for drawing me to this greatest of gifts. My life is forever changed. In Christ's name, amen.

For the grace of God has appeared that offers salvation to all people.

TITUS 2:11 NIV

DAY 329
A Witness in My Community

Lord, there are so many people in my community who either don't care about You or who think they will please You by their own merit; but several of them don't truly know You. I ask You to open doors so I may witness to them. My prayer is that many will come to You. In Jesus' name, amen.

But whoso hath this world's good, and seeth his brother have need, and shutteth up his bowels of compassion from him, how dwelleth the love of God in him?
1 JOHN 3:17 KJV

DAY 330
No Lack

I don't always get what I want, Lord, but You make sure I always have what I need. Even during my lean seasons, when the cupboard wasn't as full as I would have liked, You managed to get me through. No matter how many valleys I walk through, no matter how many deserts I traverse, You'll provide manna for the journey. I'll never come up short. You're a God of provision. With You, I will always have what I need. Thank You, Father. Amen.

The LORD your God has blessed everything you have done; he has protected you while you traveled through this great desert. The LORD your God has been with you for the past forty years, and you have had everything you needed.

DEUTERONOMY 2:7 NCV

DAY 331
As My Soul Prospers

I've walked through dark seasons in the past, and You've seen me through, Lord. There were times when my heart was so broken, I wondered if it would ever heal. My dark days even affected my health, setting me on a downward spiral of sorts. It's hard to believe I've come so far. I thank You for the healing work You've done inside of me, Father, and I look ahead with excitement. When my heart is healthy and whole (i.e., prosperous), my body will follow suit. I can walk with renewed optimism, which greatly affects my health. I want to be completely whole in You, Lord. Amen.

*Dear friend, I pray that you may enjoy good
health and that all may go well with you,
even as your soul is getting along well.*

3 John 1:2 NIV

DAY 332
Eternal Life: The Ultimate Gift

So many people in this world are quick to cut me down, Lord. They pass judgment. Bring condemnation. But not You. You're the last one to chop me to bits. In fact, You went out of Your way to do the opposite! Through the gift of Your Son, You've saved me. Sure, You want me to live a godly life. Jesus showed me how to do that—through His actions, His words, His love for others. May I be ever grateful for the ultimate gift from the God of the universe. Amen.

For God did not send his Son into the world to condemn the world, but to save the world through him.
JOHN 3:17 NIV

DAY 333
Every Good and Perfect Gift

Sometimes I forget, Lord. I forget that my belongings didn't really come from a store. My income doesn't really come from an employer. My home doesn't really come from a bank or mortgage company. All good things come from You. If it's good, if it's for my benefit, it's all You, Father. And it's all because of Your great love for us, Your kids. You desire to meet every need. May we never forget that our efforts, though good, would never be enough, if not for Your provision and Your great love. Praise You, Lord. Amen.

Whatever is good and perfect is a gift coming down to us from God our Father, who created all the lights in the heavens. He never changes or casts a shifting shadow.

JAMES 1:17 NLT

DAY 334
An Eternal Perspective

When people think of the word *prosper*, their thoughts often shift to money, lottery tickets, gold coins, jewels, fancy clothes, luxury vehicles, and so on. But You are changing our thinking about this word, Lord, and I love it. You're giving us an eternal perspective. We can't take money with us when we die. Neither can we take fine jewels nor any of the other things that the world considers prosperous. Instead of focusing on those things, today I ask that You give me an eternal perspective. Silver and gold have I none. (Well, very little anyway.) But I have a heavenly perspective that is giving me courage to walk into tomorrow with confidence. Praise You, Father! Amen.

Then Peter said, "Silver or gold I do not have,
but what I do have I give you. In the name
of Jesus Christ of Nazareth, walk."

ACTS 3:6 NIV

DAY 335
A Meek and Quiet Spirit

God, in Your economy a meek and quiet spirit is worth more than gold. It is not corruptible. It is eternal. Give me such a spirit. Make me a better listener, I pray. Set a guard over my tongue at times when I should not speak. Teach me to walk humbly with You, Father, and to serve people in Your name. A gracious, godly spirit is what You desire to see in me. Amen.

Whose adorning let it not be that outward adorning of plaiting the hair, and of wearing of gold, or of putting on of apparel; but let it be the hidden man of the heart, in that which is not corruptible, even the ornament of a meek and quiet spirit, which is in the sight of God of great price.

1 Peter 3:3–4 kjv

DAY 336
A Beautiful Work

Lord, I read of the woman who poured out a flask of expensive perfume upon Your feet. The disciples did not understand, but You saw it as a beautiful work. Give me a heart like hers. Whatever I possess, whatever comes my way, help me to fling it all forth for Your glory. Let me use it wisely but extravagantly to honor my King. I love You, Lord. Make my life a beautiful work for You. Amen.

But when his disciples saw it, they had indignation, saying, To what purpose is this waste? For this ointment might have been sold for much, and given to the poor. When Jesus understood it, he said unto them, Why trouble ye the woman? for she hath wrought a good work upon me.
MATTHEW 26:8–10 KJV

DAY 337
Shield of Faith

God, guard my heart and mind with the shield of faith. I will call on the name of Jesus when Satan tempts me. I will fight against his schemes to ruin me. My weapon is my knowledge of Your Word, promises memorized and cherished. My defense is my faith in Jesus Christ, my Savior. On this faith I will stand. Increase my faith and protect me from the evil one, I pray. Amen.

*Above all, taking the shield of faith,
wherewith ye shall be able to quench
all the fiery darts of the wicked.*
EPHESIANS 6:16 KJV

DAY 338
Iron Sharpens Iron

Lord, I find it hard to talk to my friends about areas of their lives in which they are not honoring You. And I certainly do not always appreciate their correction in my life! Father, allow such sweet, godly fellowship between my Christian sisters and me that when truth should be spoken in love, we are able to speak into one another's lives. We need one another. Iron sharpens iron. Amen.

Iron sharpeneth iron; so a man sharpeneth the countenance of his friend.
PROVERBS 27:17 KJV

DAY 339
The Value of Fellowship

Heavenly Father, I pray that You will not allow me to isolate myself. I need fellowship with other believers. I benefit from spending time with my Christian friends. You tell us in Your Word that it is not good to be alone. We need one another as we walk through this life with all of its ups and downs. When I am tempted to distance myself from others, guide me back into Christian fellowship. Amen.

*Two are better than one; because they have
a good reward for their labour. For if they
fall, the one will lift up his fellow.*

ECCLESIASTES 4:9–10 KJV

DAY 340
My Church Family

My church is special to me in so many ways, Lord. I am so thankful that You have placed me among such a wonderful group of believers who encourage me and pray for me. Allow me to be a blessing to them as well, and help me to never forget how important they are in my life. Amen.

For our comely parts have no need: but God hath tempered the body together, having given more abundant honour to that part which lacked. That there should be no schism in the body; but that the members should have the same care one for another. And whether one member suffer, all the members suffer with it; or one member be honoured, all the members rejoice with it. Now ye are the body of Christ, and members in particular.

1 CORINTHIANS 12:24–27 KJV

DAY 341
Avoiding Idleness

Lord, I know that You want me to take care of my household. Sometimes I am so tempted to put off my duties around the house, and I find myself spending too much time on the computer or the telephone. Help me to be balanced. Help me to take care of my household and to be aware of the trap of idleness. I know that procrastination is not a good or godly habit. Amen.

*She looketh well to the ways of her household,
and eateth not the bread of idleness.*
PROVERBS 31:27 KJV

DAY 342
All Hope and Peace

Of all the ways You promise to prosper me, Lord, this is one of my favorites. You are the God of all hope and peace. Wow. What good would it do to have everything I'd ever wished for, everything I'd ever dreamed of, if I didn't have hope and peace? Those two things are critical for a prosperous life. And You don't just dole out hope by the teaspoonful, Father. You pour it over me like an ocean wave! I can overflow, Lord, as I trust in You. Today I choose to do just that. Amen.

May the God of hope fill you with all joy and peace as you trust in him, so that you may overflow with hope by the power of the Holy Spirit.
ROMANS 15:13 NIV

DAY 343

Prospering: A Blessed Outcome

What a lesson this verse has been to me, Lord. I'm so quick to ask for Your blessings, but not as quick to seek Your kingdom first. Usually it's my kingdom I'm after! My desires and my will are usually top priority. Today I acknowledge that and ask for Your forgiveness. From now on, Father, may Your desires be mine as well. As I run hard after You, after Your will, I know that blessings will come. You desire to prosper me by meeting every need. But my motivation will be for You, Lord. Thanks for the timely reminder. Amen.

"But seek first his kingdom and his righteousness, and all these things will be given to you as well."

MATTHEW 6:33 NIV

DAY 344
A Watered Garden

When I think about Your plans for my life, I get so excited, Lord! I don't know what's coming next, but that's half the adventure. I do know that You are tending to every detail, even in the scorched and dry seasons. You're pouring out fresh water, saturating everything with Your Spirit. This water won't fail me, even when I'm feeling parched. You will bring hope, life, and energy to every situation. I'm so grateful, Father. Amen.

"And the LORD will guide you continually and satisfy your desire in scorched places and make your bones strong; and you shall be like a watered garden, like a spring of water, whose waters do not fail."

ISAIAH 58:11 ESV

DAY 345
Understanding His Will

Lord, I remember how as a child I didn't always understand my parents' decisions. They asked things of me that made no sense. Now, as an adult, I understand that their desires for me were good, not evil. It's the same with You, Father. Though I might not always understand Your will in the moment, You make things crystal clear to me on the opposite side. May I always seek to understand Your will, Lord, even when the road ahead appears difficult to navigate. Amen.

Therefore do not be foolish,
but understand what the will of the Lord is.
EPHESIANS 5:17 ESV

DAY 346
Desire Giver

How You love to surprise and delight me, Father! Because You know me so well, You know the little things that will bring a smile to my face. The hidden desires of my heart—the things that even my closest friends and loved ones don't know—are crystal clear to You. And You love to fulfill those desires in ways that only You can. I get a little giddy when I think about how much You love me, Lord. My greatest desire in the world is to know and love You more. Praise You, Father. Amen.

Take delight in the LORD, and he will give you the desires of your heart.

PSALM 37:4 NIV

DAY 347
Marked Out for Me

I can see it now, Lord. I'm at the starting block, just before a big race. A gunshot splits the air and I take off, light as a feather. Except this race is my life, and You're the one who has marked it out, just for me. A turn to the right, a turn to the left—You've left clear signals at the forks in the road. How grateful I am that You took the time to mark my path. As I aim myself toward You, I will keep my eye on the prize, Father. With a grateful heart, I run. Amen.

Therefore, since we are surrounded by such a great cloud of witnesses, let us throw off everything that hinders and the sin that so easily entangles. And let us run with perseverance the race marked out for us.

HEBREWS 12:1 NIV

DAY 348
A Tailored Witness

Where have You called me to go, Lord? How can I reach others for You? How can I share Your love, Your plan of salvation, with those around me? I know You've got specific places and people in mind. You haven't placed me here, where I live and work and play, by accident. You've hand-tailored my surroundings and want me to reach others in my community for You. Show me, Lord. Lead. Guide. Empower. I want to be a witness for You, Father. Amen.

"You will receive power when the Holy Spirit comes on you; and you will be my witnesses in Jerusalem, and in all Judea and Samaria, and to the ends of the earth."

ACTS 1:8 NIV

DAY 349
Straightened Paths

Okay, I'll admit it, Lord. When I make plans, they zigzag all over the place. Oh, initially they don't. I start off on the straight and narrow, but as I go along, things get a little crazy. Before I know it, what looked like a step forward becomes a jog to the right. And what looked like a simple step toward a goal becomes a complicated, dizzying journey I'm completely unprepared for. I'm so excited about the fact that You're a path straightener. Whew! You take my zigzags and turn them into a sensible road, one I can easily navigate with Your help. Thank You, Father. Amen.

*Trust in the LORD with all your heart and lean
not on your own understanding; in all your ways
submit to him, and he will make your paths straight.*

PROVERBS 3:5–6 NIV

DAY 350
Walking Out His Plan

Because I know Your plans are tailor-made for me, I can rest easy in the notion that You'll get me from point A to point B. In fact, You'll get me all the way through. You know how my feet move. You know how my thoughts ramble. You know how my ideas percolate. There's not a person on Planet Earth who knows me like You do and certainly no one capable of breathing strength into my weary bones when I feel like giving up. I submit myself to Your plans, Father, and thank You for the energy You're pouring into me today. Amen.

I can do all things through Christ,
because he gives me strength.
PHILIPPIANS 4:13 NCV

DAY 351
To Prepare a Place

It boggles my mind to think about heaven, Lord. And yet, You're already there, preparing a place for me. Your plans for me don't just include the here and now but the hereafter as well. This life of mine is well thought out, isn't it? You haven't left anything to chance. You've breathed new life into my spirit so that I can walk out Your plan here on earth and settle into my mansion in heaven once this life is through. What an amazing and generous Father You are! Amen.

"My Father's house has many rooms; if that were not so, would I have told you that I am going there to prepare a place for you? And if I go and prepare a place for you, I will come back and take you to be with me that you also may be where I am."

John 14:2–3 niv

DAY 352
For My Sake

I hear it all the time, Lord. People say things like, "I'd do anything for my family" or, "Don't mess with my kids or grandkids!" Folks are protective of their own. Lord, today I ask You to give me that kind of passion for my relationship with You. May I be so protective of my time with You, so grateful for Your plans for my life, that I fight to keep You in Your rightful place. Amen.

Jesus said, "I tell you the truth, all those who have left houses, brothers, sisters, mother, father, children, or farms for me and for the Good News will get more than they left. Here in this world they will have a hundred times more homes, brothers, sisters, mothers, children, and fields. And with those things, they will also suffer for their belief. But in this age they will have life forever."
MARK 10:29–30 NCV

DAY 353
A Way of Escape

I feel like I'm trapped in a dark alley at times, Lord, with no escape route. My own actions—well intentioned as they might be at times—take me to places that leave me feeling stuck. Oh, but how wonderful Your plans are! You always provide a way of escape for me, even when I've painted myself into a corner. Thank You for coming to my rescue, Father. I can't promise it won't happen again, but I do promise to resist temptation with Your help. Amen.

The Lord knoweth how to deliver the godly out of temptations, and to reserve the unjust unto the day of judgment to be punished.

2 PETER 2:9 KJV

DAY 354
Honoring My Parents

Heavenly Father, show me how to honor my parents. Even as I have grown into a woman, Your command remains. Give me patience with my parents. Remind me that with age comes wisdom. Help me to seek their counsel when it is appropriate. God, in Your sovereignty, You gave me the mother and father that You did. May I honor You as I honor them. Amen.

Honour thy father and thy mother,
as the Lord thy God hath commanded thee.
DEUTERONOMY 5:16 KJV

DAY 355
Use Me, Lord

Savior, You laid down Your life for me. You died a horrible death upon a cross. It was death by crucifixion, which was reserved for the worst of criminals. And You had done nothing wrong. You came into the world to save us! You gave Your very life for us. Jesus, take my life. Use me for Your kingdom's work. Only in losing my life for You will I save it. Amen.

For whosoever will save his life shall lose it;
but whosoever shall lose his life for my sake
and the gospel's, the same shall save it.

MARK 8:35 KJV

DAY 356
Serve One Another

God, I have not been put on this earth to serve myself. It is not all about me. Sometimes I forget that! Service is what this life is all about, isn't it? Father, give me opportunities to show love to others today. Make every moment a "God moment." Help me to be aware of the many needs around me. Create in me a heart that loves others and puts them ahead of myself. Amen.

By love serve one another. For all the law is fulfilled in one word, even in this; Thou shalt love thy neighbour as thyself.
GALATIANS 5:13–14 KJV

DAY 357
Putting God First

Father, a glance at my bank statement causes me to shudder. Where does my money go? Am I too concerned with what the world says I must possess to be cool, to fit in, to appear successful? Your Word says that I cannot serve both material wealth and You. I choose You, Lord. Be the master of my life and of my checkbook. I need Your help with this. Amen.

No man can serve two masters: for either he will hate the one, and love the other; or else he will hold to the one, and despise the other. Ye cannot serve God and mammon.

MATTHEW 6:24 KJV

DAY 358
No More Sorrow

Jesus, Your disciples were dismayed. You told them You were going away but that You would see them again. Those men had walked and talked with You. You were their leader, their friend. How lost they must have felt at Your crucifixion! But three days later. . . Wow! Lord, You turn mourning into rejoicing. Help me to trust in this. Thank You, Jesus. Amen.

And ye now therefore have sorrow: but I
will see you again, and your heart shall rejoice,
and your joy no man taketh from you.
JOHN 16:22 KJV

DAY 359
True Joy

Thank You, Father, for Your Word, which teaches me how to experience true joy. This world sends me a lot of messages through the media and through those who do not know You. I have tried some of the things that are supposed to bring joy, but they always leave me empty in the end. Thank You for the truth. Help me to abide in You, that I might be overflowing with joy. Amen.

These things have I spoken unto you, that my joy might remain in you, and that your joy might be full.
JOHN 15:11 KJV

DAY 360
The Inspirational Word

Lord, some mornings I wake up ready to go! I feel rested and energetic. Other mornings, I wonder how I will make it through the day. Remind me that as Your child, I have a power source that is always available to me. I may not always feel joyful, but the joy of the Lord is my strength. As I spend time in Your Word, renew my strength, I pray. In Jesus' name, amen.

For the joy of the LORD is your strength.
Nehemiah 8:10 kjv

DAY 361
Amazing Forgiveness

Lord, I come into Your presence, thanking You for forgiveness. In a culture where many experience clinical depression because of guilt, I can know my past is redeemed because of Christ's sacrifice for me. Your forgiveness is so amazing. Although I don't deserve it, You pour it out freely and lovingly. Because You have seen fit to pardon me, I bless Your name today. Amen.

In Him we have redemption through
His blood, the forgiveness of sins,
according to the riches of His grace.
EPHESIANS 1:7 NKJV

DAY 362
Fixed by His Authority

We are ruled by the clock, Lord. It tells us when to wake up, when to go to work, when to eat, when to sleep. The hours and minutes are fixed. Set. Always the same, day after day. Your times are fixed too, Lord. When You set a plan in motion, it has a timeline. And though I can't see this timeline, I can trust in the fact that it was set in place by Your authority. I can trust Your timetable, Father. I choose to trust, even when it appears to throw me off course. Amen.

He said to them: "It is not for you to know the times or dates the Father has set by his own authority."

ACTS 1:7 NIV

DAY 363
Do Not Fear

Maybe it's just my controlling nature, Father, but I have a hard time not being afraid. You ask me to take my hands off, to let You be in charge. The idea of letting go of the reins is frightening. But today I choose to let go of fear as I release my hold on the reins of my life. (They were never mine to hold in the first place, were they?) And while trusting Your plans for my life is hard, I know You will grow my faith with each step I take. I also know You're working for my good, Lord. Thank You for that. Amen.

"So do not fear, for I am with you; do not be dismayed, for I am your God. I will strengthen you and help you; I will uphold you with my righteous right hand."

ISAIAH 41:10 NIV

DAY 364
All-Seeing

My vision is so limited, Father. I can only see what's right in front of me. (And sometimes—especially when I'm looking for something specific, like my keys or phone—I can't even see what's right in front of me.) I certainly can't see what's happening one street over or in another city. Yet You see all. You are witness to every action, every word, every thought. Because You see, I can trust You, Lord. Oh, how blessed I am that my heavenly Father has twenty-twenty vision! Amen.

The eyes of the LORD are everywhere,
keeping watch on the wicked and the good.
PROVERBS 15:3 NIV

DAY 365
You Made the Day

When I ponder the fact that time is in Your hands and that You created days, hours, minutes, and seconds, I realize that each and every nanosecond is Yours to do with as You please. If You created these things, they are Yours to manage. I don't have to fret over the items on my to-do list that don't get done today, Father. All I ask is that You—my perfect, all-knowing Father—guide my steps. I will do my best to rejoice in this day, Lord, and to be happy knowing You are in control and I'm not. (Whew, what a relief!) Amen.

This is the day the LORD has made.
We will rejoice and be glad in it.
PSALM 118:24 NLT

Scripture Index

OLD TESTAMENT

New Testament

Bible Encouragement for Your Heart